Nancy —
for when the right job shows up! Jezra

Interview Like Yourself... No, Really!

Follow Your Strengths and Skills to GET THE JOB in 2014

by Jezra Kaye
President,
Speak Up for Success

Brooklyn, New York

ISBN 978-0-9793527-0-6

3Ring Press books are available at special discounts
when purchased in bulk for premium and sales
promotions as well as for fundraising or educational
use. For details, contact info@3ringpress.com

3Ring Press
191 Saint Marks Avenue
Brooklyn, NY 11238

Acknowledgements

In this book's BONUS CHAPTER, you'll find job interview tips from 64 top HR, Recruiting, and Career Coaching Professionals. I'm grateful to each of the following experts, who generously shared their wisdom and experience to help you GET THE JOB in 2014!

....

Mark P. Sneff, SPHR, Global Vice President Human Resources, Premier Research International

Caroline Ceniza-Levine, Career Expert, SixFigureStart®

Elizabeth Garone, BBC Capital Career Coach Columnist and *Wall Street Journal* Contributing Writer

Kevin M. Horan, Vice President, Human Resources and Corporate Services, International Lease Finance Corporation

Dana Manciagli, Global Career Expert, Speaker, Coach, Author of *Cut the Crap, Get a Job!*

Rob Duval, Chief Human Resources Officer, Bradley Hospital (a Lifespan Partner)

Allison Hemming, Top Gun, The Hired Guns

Celia Currin, Partner, The Art of the Career

Larry R. Reese, Sr. Vice President, Human Resources, Blood Systems, Inc.

Jennifer Bezoza, Leadership Coach, Jennifer Bezoza Consulting

Anne Loehr, Director, Anne Loehr & Associates

Daniel Poray, Director of Human Resources, Remington Hotels

Raul Argudin, Director, Human Resources, Bloomingdale's

Patrick J. Mulvey, Human Resources Consultant, PJM & Associates

Jason Leonard, VP Human Resources, Caliber Home Loans

Claudia A. Sampson, Founder/Managing Director, LEEDS Coaching

Elizabeth Cronise McLaughlin, CEO/Lead Executive Coach, Elizabeth Cronise McLaughlin Coaching

Gretchen A. Grubel, Vice President Human Resources, Hourglass Cosmetics

Linda DeCarlo, Linda DeCarlo Training and Coaching

Teauna Upshaw, MBA, PHR, Workforce Initiatives

David Almeda, Chief People Officer, Kronos Incorporated

Debra Schwartz, VP, Human Resources, HONEST TEA, Inc.

Reid Styles, VP of Human Resources, The Franklin Institute

Jim Hopkinson, *The Salary Tutor, author of Salary Tutor: Learn the Salary Negotiation Secrets No One Ever Taught You*

Darin Seeley, *Sr. Manager, Human Resources and Talent Acquisition, Black Hills Corporation*

Myles Miller, CEO & Founder, SUCCESSHQ

Joseph Terach, CEO, Resume Deli

Michelle A. Riklan, Managing Director, Riklan Resources

Sandy Lewis, VP Human Resources at Advanced Liquid Logic

Dana Harris, President, DMarie & Co.

Jean-Claude Lalumiere, Senior HR Executive

Leo Willcocks, Author of *DeStress to Success, Solving Stress and Winning Big In Relationships, Wealth and Life Itself*

Gary Glandon, Chief Human Resources Officer, Rogers Corporation

Alfred Poor, Speaker, Success Mentor, Author of *7 Success Secrets That Every College Student Needs to Know!*

Ed Chaffin, Founder/President, The UnCommon Leadership Institute

Debbie Mitchell, Human Resources Executive

Winsor Jenkins, VP, Human Resources, Northwest Pipe Company

Mike Perry, President, Szarka Financial

Samantha Lambert, Director of Human Resources, Blue Fountain Media

Jenny Gallagher, Co-Founder, Business Success

Paul Vagadori, VP Human Resources, Lahlouh

Dr. Samuel Dyer, Chairman of the Board, Medical Science Liaison Society, Author of *The Medical Science Liaison Career Guide: How to Break Into Your First Role*

Laurie Berenson, President & Certified Master Resume Writer, Sterling Career Concepts, LLC

Heidi Ferolito, Human Resources Director, Talent Acquisition and Retention, World Travel Holdings

Lynda Zugec, Managing Director, The Workforce Consultants

Ramon Santillan, Chief Interview Consultant, Persuasive Interview

Tom Gottfreid, President, Fresh Start of Illinois

Katherine Neverdousky, VP, Human Resources, American Heart Association

Lori Kleiman, SPHR, Author of *Fire HR Now!*

Evelyn Walter, GPHR, VP Human Resources, Inspirato

Parker Geiger, CEO, CHUVA group

Jason Henrichs, Managing Director, Startup Institute

Kathy Condon, Communications Author, Speaker, and Trainer

John P. Nester, Human Resources Manager

Kelly Hadous, President, Win the Room

Val Hunt Beerbower, Co-Owner, DaytonINTERNS

Cindy Allen-Stuckey, CEO, Making Performance Matter

Eileen Timmins, Ph.D., Global HR Executive, Aingilin, LLC

Dr. Michael Provitera, Author of *Mastering Self-Motivation: Preparing Yourself for Personal Excellence*

Nick Angelis, CRNA, MSN, Author of *How to Succeed in Anesthesia School (And RN, PA, or Med School)*

Mario Almonte, Managing Partner, Herman & Almonte Public Relations

Vernon Ross, Business Coach

Barry Maher, Barry Maher & Associates

David MacWilliams, Regional Director, HR, McGladrey

....

My great thanks also go to the "usual suspects," my dream team of friends, family, and advisors:

Creative Strategist **Melea Seward**, without whom there would literally be no book. Thanks for the great idea, and for guiding it, and me, every step of the way.

Business Coach **Anne Loehr**, who helps keep me on track and buttoned down.

The World's Best Virtual Assistant, **Lori Kettles**. Your warmth, humor, and can-do attitude keep me going!

Book and Cover Designer **Kit Maloney**, who makes everything she touches more beautiful.

My editing team, the wonderful **Rose Rubin Rivera**, **Mary Moreno**, **Anne Lopatto**, and **Kathi Levitan**.

And of course and always, **Jerome Harris** and **Laurika Harris-Kaye**.

Table of Contents

Introduction

This book was inspired by the many public speaking clients I've coached for winning job interviews.

Job interviews can seem overwhelming — but by and large, you already have the basic skills you need to do them well.

The task before you isn't like learning Chinese or training for a marathon. It's more about tightening up your attitude, learning simple strategies, and doing some preparation and practice. That's what this book will show you how to do.

It's divided into three easy sections:

Section 1: Get Ready...

The four chapters in this Section are about YOU. They cover things like managing fear and tapping into your natural strengths (your "super self").

You'll find many useful practices and tips in these chapters that will help you feel (and be!) more calm, powerful, and prepared to succeed.

Section 2: Get Set...

In Chapters 5 through 11, you'll learn how to **prepare** and **practice** for a job interview.

> ❯ **PREPARE** begins with learning about the job, the organization, and — if possible — the people you'll be

meeting at your interview. You'll also inventory your strengths and skills, and collect your success stories. Your final preparation step will be to figure out how you're going to answer both standard interview questions and the specific ones that you hope you're not asked.

> **PRACTICE** means working out loud on the content you've prepared until you can speak about it comfortably. It also means learning to use some basic public speaking skills that will make what you say more compelling and easier to understand.

Section 3: Get the JOB!

This section looks at your experience during the interview. You'll learn how to connect with your interviewer(s), how to handle tough scenarios like Skype or phone interviews, and how to follow up in a memorable way.

The book's final chapter is a round-up of tips from top interviewers, recruiters, HR executives, and career coaches, who'll share the one thing they wish you knew about job interviews.

But What If I Don't Have an Interview Yet?

It's never too soon to prepare for the interviews you're trying to get!

But if you've tried and tried to get through the door and haven't yet landed even one interview, here are some steps that I recommend you take:

> **Review Your Resume with an Expert.** It's almost impossible to optimize your resume by yourself. And that's not a criticism — almost no one has the objectivity you need to

boil your own career down to one or two focused, exciting, and professional-sounding pages. And the same is true for your cover letter!

In addition, your resume and cover letter should be customized for every position you apply for, because one organization may be interested in your leadership skills, while another cares more about your technical experience.

Don't put everything but the kitchen sink in a resume and expect that each organization will pull out what matters to them. Instead, focus every resume and cover letter that you send out on the words and experiences that are important for that position.

And speaking of words...

> **Do Some Research Into Key Words.** Your resume is just as likely to get its first reading from a computer as from a human being, and that computer program will, in part, be looking for the presence (or absence) of certain "key words." Search the Web for information about what words are viewed favorably in your industry, and make sure they're in your resume — preferably at the beginning of paragraphs.

> **Step Up Your Networking.** People hire people they know. Your chances of getting a job when you've been introduced to the organization by a mutual connection are vastly greater than they will be if your resume is one of hundreds that come in by anonymous email.

So activate every network you can, whether it's your high school or college alumni group; your church, synagogue, mosque, or spiritual community; every professional group you know about; friends of your friends who you find on LinkedIn, etc. (Chapter 5 has a step-by-step example of using LinkedIn to meet people who work at a particular organization or in a specific industry.)

Let people know what you're looking for. Ask their advice. Have lots of conversations. Keep telling people about your job search, your goals, and your interests; you'll be pleasantly surprised by how many people have ideas or contacts that can help you.

And last but not least...

> **Learn Everything You Can About How to Get an Interview.** While writing this book, I've discovered dozens of great web sites for job seekers, and there are literally thousands of books on the market.

There are clubs and groups, classes and courses for people who are searching, and informal Meet-Ups where you can network, support, and learn from other people who share your goal of finding work.

There is always something new to learn, and you can never know what piece of information... what contact... what lucky coincidence will help you turn the tide.

You *will* start getting interviews. And that's where this book will come in!

Section I:

Get Ready...

This book begins by focusing on YOU.

When you step into the interview room, the only thing you bring with you (except for your resume, your business cards, and maybe some breath mints) is YOURSELF, including your:

> **Skills**

> **History**

> **Attitude**

> **Personality**

> **Hopes**

> **Dreams**

> **Fears**

> **Foibles**

YOU are the best argument for hiring you, and YOU are the person who will navigate this interview.

So before we jump into technical skills like how to research an organization, answer questions, and keep a conversation going... let's get YOU ready for the challenge.

Chapter 1:
Why Are Job Interviews So ^&*(@# Hard?

You may have heard it said that getting a job is just as much work as having a job — and that's true. Job hunting is just as stressful (perhaps more stressful) than most of the jobs you'll hold throughout your life.

Why is that?

Hmmm, let's see. It could be because:

> You want something (a job), but have **little direct control** over whether or not you'll get it.

> If you're out of work, you're not earning money, so **financial stress** is also piling up.

> Your **identity and sense of self-worth** can suffer when you're not working.

The job-hunting **process can be discouraging**, and rejection (or just the fear of it) can lead to feelings of defeat, despair, even depression.

Any one of those reasons would make job hunting tough — and sometimes they're all in play. That's why job hunting, to put it bluntly, sucks.

And yet there is light at the end of this tunnel. That's because **once you get an interview, you're in a much stronger position than you think.**

What's That? You Don't Believe Me?

As a public speaking coach, I work with lots of people on their job interviewing skills.

And like many of them, some of you are probably thinking, "I'm not in a strong position!!! When I go on a job interview, *I'm the one being judged* — and that's not my idea of being in a strong position!"

Your point is taken; hence my "job hunting sucks" comment.

But the common belief that a job interviewee is completely powerless, a mere pawn in someone else's game, is just plain wrong.

On the contrary, **you got the interview because they think you're a good candidate for the job.**

This is so important it's worth repeating:

You got the interview because they think you're a good candidate for the job.

How do I know that? It's plain common sense.

These days everyone is busy, including the people who offered you the interview. So **why would they be taking time out of their busy schedules to meet with you if they didn't think you were a good fit for their job?**

The answer is pretty simple: They wouldn't.

Which means that you must be a qualified candidate — someone who would do well if you got the job.

No matter how discouraged or insecure you may sometimes feel, nobody else would waste time talking to you if **they** didn't think you had what it takes!

So as you continue reading, suspend disbelief and remember:

Once you've been invited to interview, you *are* in a strong position. You just have to learn how to leverage that strength.

TRY THIS

Stand up straight and look at yourself in a mirror.

Now repeat the following statement as confidently as you can: **"They're interviewing me because I'm a good fit for the job!"**

Now relax and take stock:

Did you look and sound confident?

> **If yes, do it again.** And if this seems corny, crazy, or childish to you, do it anyway.

> **If not, don't worry.** Keep trying from time to time, until you start to get the hang of looking and sounding like a confident job candidate.

We know from recent research that **if you look confident, you will feel more confident.** So don't hesitate to "fake it till you make it."

TO SUM IT ALL UP...

> Job interviews are hard because the stakes are high and we want (sometimes desperately) to succeed.

> If you've been invited to interview, you are — by definition — a good candidate for the job.

> If you don't feel confident that you're qualified, begin to "fake it till you make it" right now.

Chapter 2:
Fear and How to Handle It

Whether it manifests as a tortured sense of self-doubt or a full-blown case of the hives, FEAR is one of the least pleasant parts of a job interview.

But your fear is manageable. And surprisingly, it's not all bad!

Fear is Universal. How You Handle It Is Up to You.

The first thing to understand is that your fear is completely natural: You want to get this job, so why *wouldn't* you be anxious about the interview?

Studies of athletes and musicians have shown that both amateurs and professionals experience fear — and this is also true for public speakers, which is what you'll be during a job interview.

The difference is not (as amateurs often think) that professionals don't experience fear. The difference between amateurs and professionals is that *the pros have learned to take the fear they experience in stride.*

Here's what I mean:

Imagine that you're getting ready for a job interview. You're sitting at your computer researching an attractive organization that's trying to fill an interesting position — and all of a sudden, your stomach is in knots.

Or your hands and feet are numb.

Or you find yourself hyperventilating, feeling faint, or suffering from an almost overwhelming craving for ice cream, or sleep. What you say to yourself, or other people, at this moment is critical. You can say:

"I'm really scared that I'll screw up this interview and never find a good job. If I had enough self-confidence, I wouldn't be scared; so clearly I'm not qualified for this job, and it's only going to take them a few seconds to figure that out."

Or you could tell yourself (or whoever you're talking to):

"I hate how it feels when I get all shaky / achy / faint / fearful. This is ridiculous, because I'm totally qualified for the job and have nothing to be afraid of, so I'll just keep working and try to not focus on my fear."

Clearly, you're going to have a different experience if you go through Door #1 instead of Door #2 — and yet, nothing is different except your attitude toward the fear.

Which raises the interesting question:

Since fear is not a reflection of any corresponding reality ("I suck," "I'm not qualified," "I must not be well-enough prepared," etc.)... since, in essence, it means nothing except that you're afraid... why are you feeling it?

Feeling Afraid? Thank Your Amygdala!

The National Institutes of Health consider fear of public speaking — including the public speaking that's involved when you're being interviewed — a form of "social anxiety."

Social anxiety is the fear of being scrutinized or judged by others, and we all have it to some degree. We're all concerned at some level about being liked, being accepted, being respected by other people; and when those other people are interviewing us for a job, our normally low-level concerns can skyrocket through the roof.

But why does this fear become so physical? Why do we get sweaty palms or dry mouth, or experience blank minds, stuttering, or shaking?

Blame it on our amygdalas.

The amygdala (with apologies to any neuroscientists who are reading this) is the ancient area in our brain that controls our **fight-flight-or-freeze response**.

In the days when human beings survived by hunting wild animals (who were also hunting us), fight, flight, or freeze made sense. That's because we had only three ways to protect ourselves from predators: by running for the nearest tree; by fighting, with the help of a major adrenaline rush; or by holding so still that whatever wild animal was nearby didn't notice us.

And because, in those early days of our development, "danger" was immediate and deadly, it made sense for this response to be automatic — a compulsion that had to be obeyed. After all, there wasn't time to debate whether an approaching pack of hyenas was really dangerous. So when your brain said, **"Run!"**... you ran!

Times Have Changed, But Your Amygdala Hasn't

Today, that pack of hyenas is the least of your worries; and unless you live in a very bad neighborhood, most of the "danger" in your life will not be defeated by running, fighting, or holding your breath.

Unfortunately, your amygdala hasn't gotten this message. When you feel vulnerable (say, in a job interview!), it falls back on its standard **fight-flight-or-freeze** response. And since **freezing** is the only option you have in someone's office, you can end up paralyzed, tongue-tied, or blind-sided by other physical symptoms as your rational mind tries to resist the amygdala's irrational but powerful commands.

Now why, since you can't make your amygdala stop doing this, am I telling you about it?

Here's why:

If and when you feel symptoms of fear, it's important to understand that they're the result of a neutral, biological process, and **don't mean anything**.

> Fear and its symptoms don't mean that you're not prepared;

> They don't mean you're not adequate;

> And they certainly don't mean that you're not going to get the job!

They don't mean *anything* except that you care about doing well in this interview — which you already knew!

Putting Fear In Its Place

Here's something to think about: If you had a headache, you wouldn't think *that* meant you were inadequate and doomed to failure, would you?

Probably not. You would probably take two aspirin, maybe lie down for a while, and then go about your business.

That's also a good prescription for fear: Take two mental aspirin and continue whatever you're doing (with a short break first to regroup if you need one).

Mental aspirin can mean many different things. For me, a dish of ice cream can be both calming and pleasurable, but you might want to check out these less caloric alternatives:

> **Practice, Practice, Practice.** One of the best ways to combat fear is with the confidence that comes from being prepared. Give yourself the security and comfort of being prepared for every interview.

> **Try Some "Self-Talk."** A side benefit of being prepared is that you can calm yourself down by telling yourself, "I've worked hard to prepare for this interview. I'm ready to go in and give it my best."

> **Ask Trusted Friends for Support.** Just as it can help to remind *yourself* that you're a good and well-prepared job candidate, hearing it from someone else can also help calm you and connect you with reality.

> **Separate Your Feelings from the Facts.** Don't give your fear more power than it should have by thinking that it "means something." Fear is just a feeling. The fact that you're afraid **does not** mean that you're incompetent or weak, or that this job is wrong for you. It doesn't mean anything—except that you're human!

> **Accept that You're Afraid.** Sometimes, when we ignore or deny our feelings, we magnify their influence. So don't try to hide from your fear (it won't work anyway). Tell yourself that fear is a healthy and natural reaction to job interview stress, and that you can handle it.

> **Use Your Personal Tried-and-True Methods.** Like most things about job interviews, and public speaking in general, coping with fear is an intensely personal process; you have to find an approach that works for you. You may have tried techniques like the following. If they've worked for you in other situations, they can work for job interview anxiety, too:

  ◆ **Relaxed breathing** (don't do anything but breathe);

  ◆ **Light stretching** (a little burn can take your mind off... your mind);

- ◆ **Moderate exercise** (a brisk walk around the block);

- ◆ **Helping someone else** (always a great way to put your problems on the back burner); or

- ◆ **Doing something you enjoy** for a limited amount of time — a hot bath, a video game, cooking a good meal, dancing around the room, playing air guitar (or the real thing).

> **Turn Your Anxiety into Anticipation.** Tell yourself that whatever agitation you feel is *anticipation*, or even *excitement*, not anxiety (see the TRY THIS section at the end of this chapter). Research has shown that **people can interpret the same physical sensations in both positive and negative ways**, and the positive way will work better for you.

And last but not least,

> **Give In for a While**. Like most of you, I've grown up in a culture that romanticizes the "man of action" — the Bruce Willis type who overcomes all challenges through strength of will and brute force. But I've gradually realized that muscling my way through tough feelings doesn't actually work for me. What works is frequent periods of escape — in my case, with a romance novel, but you'll have your own version — before jumping back into the fray. If this works well for you, go for it. Just be sure to come out at some point and get back to work!

While you may not be able to control the sensations of fear, you *can* control what you tell yourself about them — and you can remember that fear, and its sensations, need not stop you from succeeding.

An Extra Word About Fear for "Introverts" and Shy "Extraverts"

Today, there's a greater awareness than there used to be that not everyone has the outgoing, hearty personality that's considered the ideal in our society:

> A large group of people, called **Introverts**, are more comfortable in quieter, more thoughtful, more intimate settings; and

> Even **Extraverts** who love the outer-world hustle and bustle may be shy, and habitually stay on the outer edges of the action.

If you're in either of these groups, you may have a particular dread of meeting, and making small talk with, a stranger (and that's exactly how every job interview begins).

> **Introverts** hate small talk in general, because it strikes us as shallow, and we'd rather have a deeper exchange with someone we know.

> And **shy Extraverts** (as well as shy Introverts) hate making small talk with new people because... well, you're shy!

Here's the thing, though:

You may particularly dislike small talk, but you also have the tools to do it — and to interview — brilliantly.

Your best strategy will be to treat the interviewer like someone you already know, and move quickly from the earlier, getting-acquainted phase, to the more substantive part of the conversation, where you shine.

This book will show you how to do that.

And one more thing that **everyone** should know about fear is that...

Fear Can Make Your Interview Go Better!

Here's how psychologist Alison Poulsen, PhD. explains it in an excellent blog post on performance anxiety:

"Think of how little anxiety you experience when you are sitting comfortably on your couch at home watching TV. Now imagine that you are going to perform a concert, give a speech, compete in a tournament, or go on a date. Would you want to be as stress-free as you are in front of the TV? Or would a totally relaxed, lackadaisical attitude hurt you?"

In other words, fear can sharpen your preparation, your practice, and your focus during an interview, which is a good thing.

So whether you're male or female, young or older, Introvert or Extravert, new to the job market or "seasoned," **fear — or stress, or anxiety — is a natural, and even useful, reaction to a job interview.**

Acknowledge the fear, but know that it doesn't have to get in your way. In fact, it might even help you!

.

TRY THIS

Fear isn't confined to the interview itself. As you prepare for an interview, you may find yourself experiencing symptoms of fear that include everything from slight nausea to what feels like a heart flutter, or from sweating more than usual to numbness in some part of your body.

You may well have developed ways of coping with these feelings — everything from meditation to going for a walk to calling a friend to going to a party.

Whatever fear-busting strategies have worked for you in the past, stay with them. And also try **changing the story you tell yourself about what you're feeling**.
Stories have tremendous power (we'll talk more about that in Chapter 8), so instead of making this a story about how afraid you are, try telling yourself one of these other stories:

> **Describe Your Symptoms in Completely Physical Terms.**

Instead of thinking or saying, "I'm terrified. I don't think I can do this," try telling yourself, "My stomach feels tight, and my head feels a little light. My amygdala must be working overtime." This is equally true, and has the advantage of putting some distance between you and those pesky symptoms of fear.

> **Interpret Your Physical Symptoms in a Positive Way**

Instead of thinking or saying, "I'm terrified. I'm such a loser" (or whatever you tend to think when you're scared), try telling yourself, "My body is pretty revved about this challenge. I'm looking forward to acing it." This is equally true, and has the advantage of energizing you instead of sapping your strength.

TO SUM IT ALL UP...

> Fear is a natural and universal experience that's created in a primitive part of your brain called the amygdala. Don't fall into the trap of believing that, because you're afraid, there's something wrong with you or with the way you're handling your job search. This is not true.

> Handling fear is a very personal thing. Experiment with different techniques, and think about what's helped you combat fear in the past. Know your best strategies for managing fear.

> In part, we feel fear because we interpret our physical symptoms as fear. Try interpreting them as anticipation, or as purely physical symptoms.

> Bottom line, remember that fear is an *experience* that you're having. It's not *reality*. It's not a judgment. It means nothing except that you're human.

Chapter 3:

Be Your Super Self
(Your Job Interview Avatar)

As a little kid, you probably woke up more than once wishing that you could send someone else to take a test for you, or fight that bully, or visit the dentist. (Come to think of it, there are times when we wake up as adults feeling that same way.)

Well, it turns out that — at least in the case of job interviews — there is someone you can send to take the heat for you.

That someone is **your Avatar**.

Who You Gonna Call? Your Avatar!

"Avatar" is a familiar word to anyone who plays video games or hangs out online in places where you can choose a character to represent yourself. But the idea of putting forth a more polished or confident version of yourself isn't new to the virtual age. Think about:

> **"Putting On Your Game Face"** — a phrase that means psyching yourself up to win.

> **"Persona"** — a word from drama and psychology that indicates the character you're playing.

> Even the expression **"Fake It till You Make It"** that I used in Chapter 1 shows an awareness that you don't have to feel truly and totally on top of things to give a very good impression of someone who is.

Now of course, you want to be yourself in an interview. That's why this book is titled, **_Interview Like Yourself... No, Really!_**

But that doesn't mean that you have to be _your entire, complex self, down to the last little detail._ An interview is not a court of law. You're not required to tell the truth, the whole truth, and nothing but the truth about yourself. You can tell the best parts of yourself, and leave out the ones that aren't working for you.

That's where your Avatar — **your best self** — comes in.

What's a Job Interview Avatar?

Your Job Interview Avatar is _you..._ but enhanced. It's a character, a persona, a game face, a super-hero version of yourself that is:

> **You**, with more confidence;

> **You**, but more relaxed; and

> **You**, with more of whichever of your positive qualities you'd like to have more of — and _less_ of the qualities you wish you didn't have.

That's the fun part of this game: You get to pick and choose what parts of yourself you'd like to highlight.

Then you build those positive qualities into one easy-to-invoke Avatar. (We'll get to how you do that in a minute).

Then you send your Avatar out to do the interview for you.

And the best part is that, since your Avatar is just a distillation of **the best of you** — you get to be all the good things you like most about yourself.

You get to be _your authentic best._

First, Construct Your Avatar

The best way to understand the power of an Avatar is to pick one and start getting to know him or her. Don't worry if your initial Avatar isn't perfect (there's that word again), because you can always make tweaks as you go along.

Take a minute right now to think about the 3 or 4 qualities you'd most like to embody, project, and feel when you're on a job interview. Remember, you can choose any qualities that you want, so don't hold back.

> You want competence? Check!

> Confidence? You got it!

> Intelligence? Good choice!

> Fearlessness? Friendliness? Dedication? Decisiveness?

Clearly, this could be a long list, which is why you want to pick your *top* 3 or 4 qualities.

Now **give your Avatar a name.**

As with your Avatar's qualities, his or her name isn't set in stone. If you start out thinking of him as **Go-To Guy**, or her as **Go-To Girl**, it's fine to change that to **HiPo (high potential) Girl** or **Guy** later.

The important thing is to put a stake in the ground and begin to develop your Avatar now. That way, when you need to invoke this powerful version of yourself, he or she will be familiar to you.

Now *Feel* Like Your Avatar

Once you've got a good description, it's time to start feeling like your Avatar.

You can think of this as putting on your game face, or "putting on the suit" (as the comic book and movie character Iron Man famously puts it). But I think of this process as *becoming* your Avatar, because it's not just a surface thing; it runs deep.

How do you do that? How do you feel like the Avatar you're becoming?

You pretend.

Now, pretending isn't a word that adults use much. We're supposed to be clear-eyed, hard-headed, and way too grown-up for make believe.

But think about this: When is the last time you told someone a "social lie"?

Social lies are the ones we tell to spare someone's feelings or stay out of hot water; for example:

> "You look great!"
> "This meal is delicious."
> "What an adorable baby!"
> "I'll get over it."

If you've said any of those things (or 5000 others we could list), **you know how to pretend**, because when you said those words, you were probably doing your best to mean them.

So what you're going to do now is tell a social lie *to yourself*.

You're going to tell yourself that *you feel what your Avatar feels*, whether that's confident, courageous, intelligent, or strong.

Get Your Body Into the Act

When you're practicing your Avatar, it helps to do specific, physical things, that will help you "put on the suit." These things might included:

> Sitting up straighter;
> Speaking more slowly and clearly; or
> Smiling more often.

Whether your Avatar likes to lean forward, speak more assertively, put her hands on the table, tilt his head, or whatever, making those physical gestures will help you connect with the feelings of power, competence, confidence, etc., that your Avatar embodies.

And you want to connect with those feelings often.

In fact, the best way to get comfortable with your Avatar, and be sure that he or she will always be there for you when you call, is to **always be "in" your Avatar when you're thinking about, researching, preparing, or practicing for a job interview.**

If you do this, the association will become automatic, and when something interview-related comes up, your Avatar won't be a stranger.

He or she will be ready to jump into action on your behalf.

"Fake It Till You Make It" Means Faking Out *Yourself!*

When my daughter was four, she took a standardized test to assess her readiness for kindergarten. (If you don't live in New York City, don't even try to make sense out of this!)

Since the test consisted of play tasks, my husband and I figured that our daughter would never know it was a "test" unless we told her.

So on the appointed day, we said, "Hey, guess what! We're going for a ride on the subway, and then we're going to meet a new grown-up who wants to play with you, and if she's nice and you like her, you can play with her. And if you don't want to, then we'll leave and go do something else."

This is roughly the story you want to tell yourself before a job interview:

"Hey, I'm going to go meet a new person. Maybe they'll be interesting, and if they are, we'll probably have a good conversation. And if they're not, at least I'll give it my best and then I can go do something that's fun."

Now this story leaves out a big chunk of truth (like that it's a job interview!)

But imagine if I'd told my daughter, "You're going to take a test today, and you have to be perfect, and you can't do anything wrong, and if you do we're going to punish you."

It sounds ridiculous, but many job seekers tell themselves that exact story as they travel to an interview. They think,

"I'm about to be tested big time, and I'd better not mess up! I have to be perfect, and I can't do anything wrong, and if I do, I'll be punished by not getting the job, and never getting any job, and being poor and lonely and probably homeless and..."

This is not just a depressing story to tell yourself before an interview; it's an inaccurate story, as you'll learn in Chapter 9.

Attitude + Ability = Win/Win

What all this boils down to, as I'm sure you've figured out, is to practice maintaining a powerful and positive attitude.

Of course, it's easier to have a good attitude when you're confident that you know what you're going to say and how you're going to act during your interview.

And that's what Sections 2 and 3 of this book will cover.

For now, just know that even the best job candidate in the world can sometimes suffer from a negative attitude. So if you feel yourself slipping into that trap, put the brakes on, put your Avatar on, and get back to work!

TRY THIS

What are the **3-4 qualities** you'd like to build into your Job Interview Avatar?

Write them down, or tell a friend what they are.

Now **give your Avatar a name.** (You can always change this name later if something better comes to mind.)

Close your eyes, or stand in front of a mirror, and feel the presence of those qualities in yourself. Sometimes it helps to **recite them out loud,** telling yourself, "I'm smart. I'm friendly. I'm confident. I'm [YOUR AVATAR's NAME HERE!]"

Keep on the lookout for moments when you spontaneously feel like your Avatar. **Try to notice, capture, and remember that feeling,** so that you can begin to slip back into it at will.

TO SUM IT ALL UP...

> Your Job Interview Avatar is a composite of the positive qualities you'd like to feel when you think about, work on, or do an actual job interview.

> Make your Avatar a mental and physical version of your own best qualities.

> Practice *becoming* your Avatar or, if you prefer, "putting on the suit."

> You can also "fake it till you make it" by downplaying the importance of an upcoming interview. Instead of telling yourself, "I have to do a good job," try thinking, "I'll do my best to have a good conversation with this person, and then I'll go do something fun."

Chapter 4:
The Four Job Interview Outcomes

By now, you've laid a strong foundation for the interview skills you're about to learn:

> We've established that **you're a great candidate for the job** you're interviewing for.

> You've learned about **how to manage fear**, and begun working on that process.

> You've **chosen an Avatar** — a focused blend of your best qualities — who can step forward and take charge on your behalf.

And that's just the beginning.

In the next section of this book, you'll learn how to research prospective employers, answer questions, practice for your interview, stay calm, and keep the conversation rolling.

But before we go there, let's face up to an important reality:

Job interviews, like life, are complicated, and **all sorts of things that have nothing to do with you might screw up your chance of getting hired.**

Nothing Can Guarantee You'll Get the Job

Does that sound depressing? I actually mean it in a comforting way — because if you're not completely in charge of the universe, some of the pressure to "be perfect" is off your back.

(And how do I know that you're a perfectionistic, ambitious kind of person? Because who else buys books on job interviewing techniques?!)

You can prepare for 24 hours a day. You can read 100 books. You can write the world's greatest resume. You can practice till you're blue in the face. And there's *still* no guarantee that you're going to get hired, *even if you're "perfect"* for the job!

That being the case, I suggest that you go into every interview holding two seemingly contradictory thoughts in your mind:

> **I'm going to do my best** to hit this interview out of the ballpark; and

> No matter how well I do, **the outcome of this interview is not in my control.**

Like I said, you may not enjoy this reality — I would certainly prefer to have total control of my own life! — but there are real advantages to facing it now.

The Job Interview Reality Grid

While every job interview is different, there are only four possible outcomes. I like to picture them as four squares on a game board, hence the name "Reality Grid."

Here are the four things that can happen. Two of them assume that you executed the interview to the best of your ability ("You interviewed well") and two assume that you weren't on your A game ("You didn't interview well").

In these two outcomes, YOU GET THE JOB:

1 **You interview well AND you get the job** (or at least get moved up to the next round of interviews). **YAY!! Celebration!! Fireworks!!! You did it!!!**

2 **You don't interview well BUT you get the job anyway** (or at least get moved up to the next round of interviews). Whew!!! CONGRATULATIONS! For some reason, you lucked out on this one. Maybe your kick-ass credentials saved the day, but whatever happened, be grateful for it.

In these two outcomes, YOU **DON'T** GET THE JOB:

3 **You don't interview well AND you don't get the job.** Well, that's not too surprising, is it? At least you know how to improve your chances of doing better in your next interview: Start working on your interviewing skills now!

4 **You interview well BUT you don't get the job.** When this happens to you (because it almost certainly will, at some point), remember that a job interview is kind of like a first date:

◆ If you're serious about finding a mate, you'll probably have to go on lots of first dates and suffer some disappointments.

◆ Same thing if you're serious about finding a job. You may have to go on many job interviews, and probably suffer some disappointments before you find the organization you can "settle down" with.

But here's the good news:

Once you've found the job (or partner) **who's right for you and returns your feelings**, it won't matter how many disappointing interviews (or bad dates) you went on.

Those things will be forgotten in the joy of finally getting what you want!

OK, Nice Pep Talk! But WHY Would I Not Get the Job if I Interviewed Well?

You're never going to really know — but *do* know that it may have NOTHING to do with you.

Among the umpteen things that can go wrong with even a great interview are:

> **The "Fix" Is In.** In this frustrating case, the organization has an inside candidate that they know will get the job, but they have to go through the motions of interviewing other people because HR (the Human Resources department), or Procurement (the people who hold the purse strings), or some powerful executive demands it. In this situation, the outcome is predetermined and not even the world's most brilliant interview will change things in your favor.

> **The Absolutely Perfect Candidate Comes Along.** You were their #1 choice until that woman who speaks Polish *and* American Sign Language showed up. They were willing to teach you Polish because you're such a great candidate, but now they don't have to.

> **Your Interviewer Loved You, but Everyone Else Hates Him.** Sometimes, through no fault of your own, you end up with an advocate who does you more harm than good. If two different interviewers are promoting two different candidates and your interviewer is the less powerful or less popular of the two, you can be stone cold out of luck in spite of your stellar interview.

> **The Job Goes Away.** Just because an organization is interviewing people for a job doesn't mean that the job is locked and loaded, or that conditions won't change during the hiring process. You'd be surprised at how often this happens. And no matter how well you interview, you can't get hired for a job that isn't there.

By now, you get the moral of this chapter:

Since we're not in charge of the universe, we can't control how things will turn out. So let go of the pressure to be perfect...

Study the game plan in this book...

And keep putting one foot in front of the other until that happy day when you get a great job!

TRY THIS

Think about (or write about, or talk to someone about) **an area of your life where you tried many times to do something before succeeding.** Sports provides some great examples, but this could also be a personal quest, like getting back in shape; or a professional one, like passing a certification test.

Do you remember **how you felt when things didn't work out** the first, or second, or maybe even the third, fourth, or fifth time?

What helped you keep going until you reached your goal?

Whatever tips, tricks, and attitude enhancers you learned from this experience, dust them off and **get ready to use them** in your job hunt.

They've helped you win in the past, and **they will help you win again.**

TO SUM IT ALL UP...

> There are only four job interview outcomes: Either you'll have a good interview, or you won't. And either you'll get the job, or you won't. You don't have the power to change this simple fact.

> If you're not happy with your job interview performance, keep studying this book, and practicing.

> If you don't get hired for a particular job, *the reasons may have nothing to do with you.* Remind yourself that you did your best, and that a better break will come along soon.

Section 2:

Get Set...

In Section 1, you **got yourself ready** for the job interview process.

Now, in Section 2, I'll show you how to **prepare for interviews**.

Interviews are a cross between small talk and Q&A, but the central activity is almost always answering questions. You'll learn how to research an organization so that you know what's of value to them... how to "research" yourself, so you know what you bring... and how to answer questions in a way that works.

You'll also learn how to make a **Statement**, tell **Success Stories**, and create **Instant Speeches** using a short form that adds weight and authority to any discussion.

Ready to roll up your sleeves? Let's go!

Chapter 5:

Know Your Target
(How to Research the Organization and Interviewer)

Here's a story that was told back in the day when IBM was the best organization in the world to work for. (Yes, I go that far back!)

A guy who was just graduating from college got an interview at IBM. Being kind of a jerk, he bragged to all his friends that he was as good as hired and was going to rise through the ranks, become a powerful executive, and get rich.

On the day of his interview, the interviewer started with this question: "What do the letters IBM stand for?"

The young man didn't know, and he didn't get the job — because IBM figured that it didn't need to hire someone who couldn't be bothered to research their company. (Answer: International Business Machines)

"Research" is Like a Treasure Hunt

Lots of people hate the idea of research. Based on our school days, we see it as a thankless task that's going to eat up all our free time, complicate our work to no real purpose, and lead to lots of dreaded footnotes.

But that's not what *this* research is going to be like.

Job search research is more like going on a treasure hunt. Yes, you want to learn things, but that's not the main goal. Your main goal is to find:

> Things that you can talk about during your interview; and
> Clues about what the organization is looking for.

Here are some places you can go hunting for that buried treasure.

The Interview Invitation

It may be a form letter. It may be an email. It may be three sentences long. No matter. Scour it for details, particularly:

> **The name, title, and department of the person who's interviewing you.** Are they from the HR (Human Resources) department? If not, it's likely that they're part of the team you want to join. Memorize (or at least get very familiar with) any name mentioned in your invitation. You want to address the interviewer correctly when the time comes.

> **If you're going to be interviewed by several people, see if you can figure out which one of them will be making the decision to hire.** Sometimes their titles will tell you this, and it's great to know in advance. But if you can't figure it out now, don't worry. You'll be able to tell at the actual interview (the person that everyone else defers to is the decision-maker).

The Job Description

Let's go out on a limb and assume that the job description that was posted for the position you want is accurate. (It could be inaccurate for lots of reasons, including careless writing or changing conditions at the organization.)

The job description is filled with things you may be asked about, such as requirements and qualifications.

You've already addressed these areas in your resume and cover letter; now you'll prepare to *talk* about them in your interview.

The Organization's Web Site

Make two trips through the organization's web site.

First, scour it for **facts**. These might include the age of the organization, the places where it operates, the lines of business it's in, the number of employees, etc.

If you're good with facts, you'll remember much of what you learn on this pass — but **take notes** anyway!

And if you're not good at retaining facts, don't worry; use them to get a more general picture of the organization's size and the scope of its activities.

Once you've done that, make another complete pass through the web site looking for **soft information about the organization's culture**.

Check out the web site's colors, pictures, and writing. Are they conventional, or quirky? Crisp, or warm and fuzzy?

What kinds of stories are told on the web site, and what values do they suggest? Does the organization want you to know that it's a good neighbor? A ruthless competitor? A force for change? A guardian of tradition?

If you're good at reading between the lines, you may learn more from this "reading" of the web site than from the first one.

And if you're not good at intuiting things, don't worry; use this pass to get a general impression of the organization's personality.

LinkedIn

As I write this, LinkedIn is the world's largest publicly available directory of who works where, and who they know.

If you have a LinkedIn profile (and if you don't, you should!), a LinkedIn search will also return information about the connections that you and various people of interest have in common.

Here's an example of how that can be useful when you're trying to learn more about an organization:

My daughter's best friend Karla is interested in working at a particular mid-sized media organization, so we used my account and did a **LinkedIn search for people who work for that organization** (let's call it "Acme").

> LinkedIn returned hundreds of names of people who work for the organization in various positions around the world. (We could have narrowed our search geographically, but chose not to.)

> Of those hundreds of people, LinkedIn told us that **66 Acme employees know someone that I know.** We used my account for this example, since Karla is relatively young and I have more LinkedIn connections. But she searched LinkedIn using her own account, too.

> Looking more closely at those 66 people, I quickly determined that **five Acme employees who have positions that are relevant to Karla's interests are connected to me** *through someone that I know well.* This is important, because you may be connected through LinkedIn to people you only know casually, or don't know at all.

Do you see how this works?

In just minutes, I came up with five people who would be easy to reach (through our close mutual connections); who have jobs that my friend Karla wants to know more about; and who (again, because we have close mutual connections) are likely to be willing to talk to her.

That's the beauty of LinkedIn. And even though this was an exploratory exercise, it works even better when you have an actual interview.

Why? Because **if you already have an interview, you already have the name of someone from that organization** (the person who contacted you). Since this is the case:

> **Go onto LinkedIn and read that person's profile.** Can you get a sense of their personality? Their job duties? Their approach to doing business?

> **Are there questions you'd like to ask this person?** Do you see any areas of commonality? If they are the "gatekeeper" (the person organizing your interview) rather than the person who will interview you, do they seem like someone you could approach to ask who your interviewer will be? (Example: "John, is it possible for me to find out who will be interviewing me next week? I'd like to be well prepared for the interview, and any information you can give me is much appreciated. Thanks, Karla.")

Once you've learned what you can about your contact,

> **Do a LinkedIn search on the organization's name** and (if it's a giant or global corporation) the location where you'll be interviewing:

> **Note the names of people you may want to meet**, and particularly the ones who are 1st or 2nd degree connections, meaning (in LinkedIn terms) that you're either connected to each other directly, or connected to each other through one person that you both know.

> **Note job titles and how work at the organization seems to be organized.**

> **Get whatever sense you can of the organization's culture**, by noting how people present themselves and describe their jobs.

If you're someone who's easily overwhelmed by information, resist the temptation to get overwhelmed (re-read Chapter 2 if you need to), and notice *how much better informed* about this organization you now are.

There's no guarantee that the information you've collected will benefit your interview. But it only took minutes to gather and, as a friend of mine is fond of saying, "Can't hurt, might help!"

Search Engines

It's easy to think that once you've probed the organization's web site and researched its employees on LinkedIn, your research is finished. But the organization's web site and employees' LinkedIn profiles only tell you how the organization and its employees *want to be perceived.*

There are **lots** of things an organization will not tell you on its web site — things that may directly affect your interview, and even the job you hope to fill. In addition, whenever you're trying to understand something (be it a topic, an organization, a news item, whatever), you're better off coming at the subject from multiple points of view and perspectives, because the truth is usually a blend of points of view.

So take your research efforts to the Internet at large (and to your real world contacts, too; but let's talk Internet first).

Here are some questions to explore with the help of a good search engine:

> Has the organization been through any **big changes** in the last year or so?

> Have they launched any new **products** or started to explore **new lines of business**? Have they moved into any **new geographic areas**?

> Is the **financial news** about them positive?

> Have there been any big changes in **leadership**? Any **scandals**? Any **other issues** that they might be sensitive about?

> Is there any **recent news** or general information about the area you want to work in? How about the people who'll be interviewing you?

> **What else** can you learn about the organization, your prospective team, and your interviewers?

Other Social Media Sites

Check every site you're familiar with (LinkedIn, Facebook, Twitter, Pinterest, and any others that you know about) for information about your interviewer and the organization.

And remember, information can be personal as well as professional.

What if it turns out that the person who's interviewing you grew up in your home town? Or plays your favorite sport? Or has kids who are the same age as your kids?

Again, whether or not you mention these connections during your interview, it's good to "have them in your back pocket."

Word of Mouth: Tap Your Personal Connections

Now that online data is abundant, and searches are easy to perform, it's easy to forget that people are still your best potential source of information.

People bring a whole new dimension to your research. You can ask them questions. They can find things out for you. And they can give you advice, or interpret the facts in a way that may not have been obvious when you read them online.

Where do you find people to talk to?

> You may know **someone who used to work at the organization** you want to work for.

> The person who'll be interviewing you may be **Facebook friends** with a friend of yours.

> You may have **a contact who's an expert on the industry** or the type of job you're applying for, even if they don't know anything about this particular organization.

> **People that you've worked with in the past** may be willing to share their thoughts about the situation you're exploring.

> And don't forget that **all those potential connections you discovered on LinkedIn** (people who know someone who knows you) may be willing to have actual conversations that will provide you with insights and information.

So reach out to *everyone* who knows something that might be relevant to your job interview, and ask to speak with them about the organization, its culture, what people are saying about it, and most of all, the individuals you'll be interviewing with and hopefully working for.

You never know where a valuable contact, fact, or key insight is going to come from.

And speaking of that...

Look Beyond Your Own Level

Let's say that you're going to be interviewing for a position as a Senior Manager.

It might be tempting to think that the only people who can give you insights into the organization you want to join are at or above the Senior Management level (meaning other Senior Managers, Vice Presidents, Senior or Executive Vice Presidents, and C-Suite executives like the CEO, CFO, CIO, COO, CMO, etc.)

Getting input from folks at or above your level is a great thing, but don't think for a minute that they're the only sources it makes sense to tap. Consider:

> **Executive Assistants** — The good ones are as smart as executives, and because they keep a low profile and are trusted with every aspect of the organization's business, they may be better informed about what's really going on than their bosses are.

> **Direct Reports** — Nobody understands a boss like the people who report to him or her. If you want to work for that same executive, find out what he or she is really like from the people who know best.

> **Internal Clients** — These are the people within the organization who'll be evaluating your work if you get the job. They know what it takes to succeed in your hoped-for new position.

If you have connections to any of these folks, don't pass up a conversation just because they aren't "at your level."

TRY THIS

It's important to keep track of the information you'll find as you begin to research an interviewer and/or organization. So find a system that's easy to use before you start what may turn out to be a major research project.

Among the systems I've seen put to good use are:

> A **spreadsheet**;

> Your **Contacts** program (put information about people in the Notes section);

> A **Word or Pages document** into which you cut and paste everything you want, so that it serves as a record of your research effort;

> **A wall for pasting up all your notes**, whether they're on print-outs, scraps of paper, business cards, whatever.

> **A CRM** (customer relationship management) software program that will allow you to keep everyone's contact info, store the emails that you send and receive on each person's record, and pull up everyone who's in a particular organization. I use Highrise HQ. They have a free version that you'll find if you read the fine print on their Plans and Pricing page.

Pick one of these systems, or another one I haven't thought of, and do a "dry run" research project.

Does your system work? Great!

If not, now's the time to tweak it or look for another, because you don't want to be thinking of this when you're deep in the weeds of preparing for an actual interview.

TO SUM IT ALL UP...

> Use every research tool you can, including the job description, organization's web site, social media, and an Internet search.

> Cast a wide net, because you never know what will be useful when you're in the actual interview.

> Don't overlook real people as a source of insight and information. If you know anyone who knows anyone who's connected to the organization you want to join, try to talk with them.

> Keep your information in good order so that you can find what you need when you need it. That way, you won't have an additional reason to panic.

Chapter 6:
Anticipate the Questions They're Going to Ask

Did you ever play an old word game called **20 Questions**? It works like this:

> Someone thinks of an **object** (anything from an Xbox to an elephant).

> The other players have to figure out what that object is by asking **no more than 20 "yes or no" questions** (in other words, only questions that can be answered with yes or no are allowed, such as: "Is it bigger than a table?" "Is it bigger than a house?" "Is it alive?" "Is it used for entertainment?")

In a way, your interviewer is playing this game. He or she starts with a "universe" (or at least a pool) of possible people to hire, and asks questions that will hopefully narrow down their search to one person.

What are the questions you're most likely to be asked?

This chapter is about how to figure that out.

After all, you can't work on your answers to questions if you don't have at least a tentative list of the questions that may come up during your interview.

Four Types of Questions

I've organized the questions that you're likely to be asked during an interview into three categories. These categories aren't based on the content of the questions (past jobs, professional goals, hobbies, etc.), but rather on how *you're* likely to experience them:

> **Generic Questions.** These general questions are so open-ended that any interviewer in the world could ask them of any job candidate. Most people experience these questions as mysterious and/or frustrating.

> **Job-Related Questions.** These are the opposite of generic questions, and the easiest to prepare for. They ask about the specific skills and work experiences that are relevant to the particular job you're interviewing for. (If the job is "financial analyst," you expect to be asked about your knowledge of statistics, right?)

> **Awkward Questions.** These questions are also specific, but in a way that makes them more difficult to answer. They touch on the weaknesses, ambiguities, gaps, or holes in your experience — the sore spots that you probably have mixed feelings about. Not every interviewer will notice, or zero in on, your particular vulnerabilities but you have to be prepared in case they do.

> And finally you'll need a list (for each interview) of **Questions that *You* Ask Your Interviewer.** You'll ask these questions because you want to know the answers, but also (and perhaps more importantly) to show your interviewer that you're sincerely interested in this job and have done your homework to learn about the organization.

Pick One Interview, and Prepare a List of Questions

Your task, for the rest of this chapter, will be to **prepare a list of sample questions** that you might be asked during an interview.

But since you'll probably have many different interviews, let's narrow that down by picking **one real or imagined interview** from all of the possible interviews that you've done... that you're scheduled to do... or that you hope to be able to do in the future.

And yes, this does mean that you'll be doing this exercise for each interview, because there is no one-size-fits-all list of questions for every interview.

So for now, focus on the sample interview you've chosen to prepare.

If you have already researched this company, you're ahead of the game. If not, your choice is to do that research now, before going further into this chapter, or to *imagine* details that enable you to create a question list.

Either approach is fine for now. Just be sure, when a real interview comes along, that your preparation for it is based on real research!

Generic (General) Questions

While you can always hope that an interviewer will be better prepared and more creative, you need to be ready for generic questions. Again, these are questions that could be asked of anyone, in any situation.

A recent survey of thousands of HR professionals found that the five questions they were most likely to ask are:

> "Tell me a little about yourself."

> "Why did you leave your last job?"

> "What do you know about our organization?"

> "Why do you want to work for us?"

> "Tell me about your experience at _____."

Other generic questions that have bedeviled job seekers include:

> "Where do you see yourself in five years?"

> "Why should we choose you?"

> "What is your greatest weakness?"

> "Describe a time you succeeded/failed at something complex/challenging/major."

> "What is your style of leadership?"

> "Are you a team player?"

> "What is an obstacle that you have overcome?"

These questions are difficult to answer precisely because they're so general that they turn your brain to mush.

As an example, If I ask you to tell me your worst high school experience, you can probably bring something to mind. But if I ask, "Tell me about high school," it's entirely possible that nothing — good, bad, or indifferent — will occur to you, because the question is just too general.

For this reason, there's a trick to answering generic questions: You **don't answer the literal question that was asked**. You speak, instead, to *what you think your interviewer really wants to know.*

You'll learn how to apply that approach in the next chapter. But for now, just make a list of the generic questions you might be asked during your sample interview.

This list (like the questions themselves) will be arbitrary, so don't try to find **the most likely** questions. Instead:

> **Think about your research** into this organization

> Based on what you've learned (say, they're proud of their values; or they're aggressively competitive) **make up a**

few possible questions (such as, "What is your most important value?" or "How would you describe yourself as a competitor?")

> **Write these questions down**, and move onto the next, easier step!

Job-Related Questions

Unlike generic questions, job-related questions are likely to be specific and self-explanatory.

Your research on the organization, job, and interviewer will pay off as you brainstorm questions that you expect to be asked about how well you would do *this particular job*. (Again, there is no one-size-fits-all list of questions to prepare.)

Write down potential job-related questions, including:

> **Your skill set.** If this job involves *a body of technical knowledge* (whether that's systems integration or 17th century French literature), you'll almost certainly be asked about it. So write down some questions (a few easy, a few tough) that test your grasp of the relevant subject matter.

> **Soft skills.** Your interviewer may ask questions about your approach to management, leadership, or teamwork. ("What's your approach to...?") But you may also be asked open-ended questions ("What did you do in your last position?") that give you the *opportunity* to tell stories about your approach to management, leadership, or teamwork. In Chapter 8, you'll learn how to tell these stories. For now, just write down some questions that, directly or indirectly, inquire about your *soft skills*.

> **"What if...?" questions.** Instead of asking what you've *done*, these questions ask you to address problems that you might encounter if you get this job, such as: "What would you do if the deadline was 9AM tomorrow and three of your

key people were out sick?" or "What would you do if a client got hysterical and started screaming at you?"

Questions like these are intended to gauge your working style, but also your knowledge of the **organization's culture**. (Some companies want you to suck it up with the screaming client; others expect you to call in your supervisor.) We'll talk about that in the next chapter; for now, to be sure that you're prepared for **Job-Related Questions**, write at least ten questions that you might be asked in your sample interview.

Awkward Questions (The Ones You Hope You're Not Asked)

We all have *areas of ambivalence or embarrassment* in our work backgrounds. And if there seem to be *technical or soft skills "gaps"* in your resume, many interviewers will focus on them.

You should do the same in advance of your interview. Here are some examples of questions that many of us would find awkward to answer:

> "Why haven't you been working for the last three years?"
> "Why did you leave your last position?"
> "Will you move if your spouse gets transferred again?"
> "Aren't you surprised you haven't been promoted by now?"
> "You have very little hands-on experience. Why is that?"

No one likes to be put on the spot, and it's tempting — though useless — to act as if we can avoid these questions by sticking our heads in the sand, ostrich-style, and pretending they don't exist.

Unfortunately that magical thinking doesn't work. Of course you're going to be asked about the unusual, irregular, or ambiguous things in your resume. Finding red flags that might eliminate you is part of an interviewer's job.

So write down **every question you can think of that you don't want to be asked.** These are the hardest questions to answer, and in Chapter 7, you'll learn how to approach them.

For now, dig deep into your most embarrassing back pages and shine the light of day on every awkward or embarrassing question — or at least, put it on your question list!

Your Questions for the Interviewer

One of the best ways to connect with your interviewer is to ask interesting questions.

Your questions can be about any aspect of the organization, or job: R&D, culture, future plans for growth, etc. And it's fine to show you've researched the organization — that's what they expect you to do — by asking questions like:

> "I read that you just opened a state-of-the-art laboratory. What kind of science will be done there?"

> "Now that you've acquired DataGen, will Software-as-a-Service still be a major focus for your organization?"

> "On your web site, I saw that you stress helping the local community. That's something I value, and I wondered if all of your employees do community service projects."

Don't, however, ask a question that shows you *haven't* researched the organization, such as, "Have you made any interesting acquisitions lately?" (A quick news search on the company name would have revealed the answer to that one!)

Toward the end of your interview (and we'll talk more about this in Chapter 13), it's also fine to turn the tables on your interviewer by asking for opinions, such as,

> "What do you like best about working here?"

> "Your organization seems to have a relaxed culture, but incredibly productive people. How does that happen?"

> "If I'm lucky enough to get this position, what advice would you give me for succeeding in it?"

Your Lists of Questions Will Help You Find Answers

In the next three chapters of this book, you'll continue to explore job interview **questions**, and how to answer them.

Obviously, that work will be more valuable if you have a list of even hypothetical questions at hand.

So if you haven't already created that list, why not create it before you read on!

TRY THIS

Before we go on, do a quick "pretend" exercise that puts you briefly into an interviewer's shoes. (Trust me, there's a point to this!) Here's how the game is played:

> Either **invite a friend** to help with this exercise or imagine that someone else is playing the part of "you." (You can play both parts, if you'd like.)

> Now sit down at a desk or table, and **take out the interview questions** that you prepared while reading this chapter.

> Pick any question, and **ask it in your best "I'm an interviewer" style.**

> Now **whoever's playing "you" (the person being interviewed) answers the question.** The point is not

that they answer the question well, just that they're talking.

> While they're talking, you (the interviewer) will be (a) listening to the other person's answer, (b) taking notes on what they say, (c) trying to "hear between the lines" in case there are red flags or things you should follow up, and (d) picking your next interview question. **Do these things simultaneously**, while maintaining a pleasant demeanor and a respectful, neutral attitude toward the person who's talking.

> **Keep this up for at least 4 or 5 rounds** of questions and responses.

Not so easy, is it? Interviewing can be hard work!

But you can make things easier for your interviewer by being prepared, by anticipating what you may be asked, by having reasonable answers ready, and by helping the conversation to flow.

None of that is easy, either! But if you're well-prepared, and trying to make the interviewer's job easier, two interesting things will happen:

You'll feel stronger, and your interviewer will appreciate the help.

TO SUM IT ALL UP...

> The questions that are likely to come up in any interview can be classified as: Generic Questions; Job-Related Questions; Awkward Questions; and Your Questions for the Interviewer.

> **Generic Questions** could be asked of anyone, in any interview. They are particularly hard to answer off-the-cuff, so try to anticipate as many of them as you can.

> **Job-Related Questions** will be focused on the specific skills and experiences the organization requires for this particular job, including "soft" skills like the ability to work on a team.

> **Awkward Questions** require thought, not because they're hard or obscure but because they're embarrassing. You might want to avoid these questions, but it's important to anticipate them.

> **Your Questions for the Interviewer** are critical. Don't miss this opportunity to show your interviewer that you've done your homework, and care about getting this job.

Chapter 7:

How to Master the Fine Art of Answering Questions

There are three basic ways to answer questions.

The simplest is to **answer with a Statement**.

This is a great approach to answering questions of fact, such as "What year did you graduate?" (1993); "Are you familiar with Six Sigma?" (No, I'm not. What is it?) or "What do the letters IBM stand for?" (International Business Machines).

Of course, even the simplest Statement should meet certain criteria — and that's what we'll focus on in this Chapter.

But sometimes, an effective answer requires more than one or two sentences. So as you work through this chapter, don't be concerned if the approach that it describes doesn't apply to all of your questions.

In Chapter 8, we'll look at two other techniques that, together with simple Statements, will let you answer any question: Success Stories (which are great for telling... stories!) and Instant Speeches (for when you need to discuss or argue a point, or sound more expert or authoritative).

For now, though, let's look at how to answer questions with a Statement.

Whoa, Aren't We Getting a Little Obsessive about How to Answer Questions?

It may feel that way, but consider this:

Answering questions (whether it's with Statements, Success Stories, or Instant Speeches) is the **core** of what you'll be doing in an interview. That makes it a good place to invest some time and energy.

And here's the thing: **Very few people can answer high-stakes questions in a relaxed, friendly, and positive way without preparing in advance.**

Sure, you've seen celebrities and politicians keep their cool while reporters throw rapid-fire questions at them. But that just makes my point, because *politicians and celebrities have prepared!*

They have publicists. They have coaches. They have practiced, sometimes for most of their lives, to sound cool, calm, and collected in the face of public pressure.

You haven't — which is why you're going to do it now! And the point of this book is *not* to turn you into an obsessive nerd who can't talk without thinking about the four types of questions and the three ways to answer them.

The point is to explore this skill set **now** so that *you don't **have to** think about it* (or worse, flounder helplessly) when you're in an actual interview.

What's Your Goal When You Answer Job Interview Questions?

Interestingly, your goal is not — as many people assume — to:

> Just **answer the question** (more on that in a minute);
> **Impress the interviewer** (you can't control what he or she thinks of you);

> **Make him or her like you** (you can't make that happen, though it's certainly worth a try);

> Be **cooperative** (of course, cooperate; but don't work so hard at being nice that you give up control over how you're going to answer questions); or

> **Defend your credentials** (you wouldn't have this interview if you weren't qualified for the job; if you're in any doubt about that, please re-read Chapter 1).

Focusing on those things is a waste of your valuable time and attention, for the reasons we discussed in Chapter 4 (The Four Job Interview Outcomes). So what is your goal, when you're answering job interview questions?

Your GOAL is to demonstrate that you're the person they should hire.

Repeat: **Your GOAL when you answer job interview questions is to demonstrate that you're the person they should hire.**

You do that by giving answers that (a) satisfy your interviewer's concerns, while (b) putting yourself in the best possible light.

Of course, before you can "satisfy your interviewer's concerns," you'll have to understand what those concerns really are — in other words, what he or she *really* wants to know.

What Are Generic and Awkward Questions Really Getting At?

When you're asked a job-related question ("What's your best programming language?"), it's pretty easy to see what information that question is designed to reveal. But generic and awkward questions are more opaque, because there's often *another question* lurking beneath the one that was asked.

To illustrate this point, let's deconstruct three generic and awkward questions:

 It's possible that the world's most-hated generic question is, **"Tell me a little about yourself."**

Does your interviewer *really* mean, "Please pick any old thing to tell me, because I would be interested in hearing *absolutely anything* you want to share about your life"?

Not for a minute! What he or she *really* means is, "Tell me something about yourself *that shows whether or not you fit what we're looking for in the person we hire.*"

Believe it or not, that's an easier question to answer, because thanks to your research, you have a pretty good idea of what they're looking for.

 This one is an awkward question: *"Why did you leave your last job?"*

As you can imagine, this question should almost never be answered with the truth, the whole truth, and nothing but the truth.

That's because, although *you* know that your criticisms of your last organization are fair, your interviewer *doesn't* know that any sane person would have left the place, just like you did. This discrepancy (between what's obvious to you and what's unknown to him or her) leaves way too much room for your interviewer to decide that you're a complainer, a crackpot, or someone who doesn't have team spirit.

So how do you answer a question like this one?

Start by thinking about your GOAL, which is **to demonstrate that you're the person they should hire.**

With that in mind, it's likely that what your interviewer *really* wants to know is, "Are you a complainer, a crackpot, or someone who doesn't have team spirit?"

If that's true, your best strategy is to say very little, and say it very diplomatically. A perfect example would be, "After five years with the organization, I was ready for a new challenge."

This politically correct response answers *the question behind your interviewer's question* by demonstrating that you can be trusted to not badmouth the people you've left behind — no matter how much you think they deserve bad-mouthing!

And notice that you're "allowed" to give a generic answer to a generic question. Sometimes, as in this case, you have very little choice!

3   OK, one more typical generic question:
       "What is the biggest challenge you've overcome at work?"

Again, don't get into lots of detail about how challenging things were on your last job, because that's not the real point. The *real* point is for you to share something that reveals how you react under extreme stress.

This is one of those questions that you can answer with a Success Story, and we'll talk about how to turn *stress* into *success* in Chapter 8.

For now, though, notice that the question behind this question is probably, ***"Tell me something about how you react under extreme stress that demonstrates why should we hire you."***

Come to think of it...

Every Interview Question Translates Roughly Into "Why Should We Hire You?"

Once you realize that this is the **primary concern** behind almost all of the questions you'll be asked, it will be easier to choose your answers. Test this by picking an answer to the following three questions:

1 **"Tell me something about yourself."**

    a. "I was born in a suburb of Boston, Massachusetts, and grew up with three younger siblings who I'm still very close to."

    b. "I've always loved technology, but when I went to college my folks really wanted me to study business. That's how I ended up getting an MBA and a Masters in Computer Science, which turned out to be the best decision I ever made."

2 **"Why did you leave your last job?"**

    a. "After five years with the same organization, I was ready for a new challenge."

    b. "I was moved into a new position, and my new boss was a highly controlling micro-manager. He and I just couldn't work together, so it was time for me to go."

3 **"What is the biggest challenge you've overcome at work?"**

    a. "One time, my VP of Sales had to have emergency surgery, and she asked me to take the lead on a major pitch that was happening the next day. It was pretty nerve-wracking, and last minute pressure isn't my favorite thing. But it went great, and we got the job."

    b. "It was hard to keep up with the work flow in my last position. There were always last-minute demands, and very little guidance on how to prioritize the work."

The answers that best achieve your GOAL of demonstrating that you're the person they should hire are B, A (with a caveat), and A.

Interestingly, though, there are two different strategies at work here.

> In Questions 1 and 3, which invite you to share something positive about yourself, answers B and A work best because they're more detailed and specific.

> However in Question 2, which invites you to hang yourself with the rope that's thoughtfully being provided, answer A is the right choice because it says less than Answer B — with a caveat.

That caveat is: if you believe that you've established enough credibility and rapport with the interviewer to make it worth taking this risk, the candid but respectful tone of Answer B could also work for you.

As a **general** rule, however:

> **When a question asks for positive information**, be specific and give details. You can also give positive answers to performance-related questions that sound negative ("...the hardest thing..." or "a time when you failed...") by talking about how much you learned from the experience!

> **When a question invites you to go negative about other people** ("Why did you leave?" or "Have you ever had a conflict with a boss?"), don't do it! Instead, keep your answer short, sweet, and as general as possible.

A Few More Guidelines for Your Statements

We've talked about how to meet your GOAL of **demonstrating that you're the person they should hire,** and we've taken a look beneath the surface of some generic and awkward questions to see what the interviewer really wants to know.

Here are a few more things that will make your Statements as strong as possible, whether they're one sentence long or, like some of the examples in this chapter, more elaborate.

> **Answer your interviewer's question first.** If I ask you whether you graduated from college, do not reply, "Let me explain what things were like back when I was in school. My father had just had a heart attack..." Instead, answer the question first, and then put your answer into perspective. You might say, "No, I dropped out in my third year to take care of my Dad," or "No, I never graduated, but I had a 3.3 GPA when I left and I plan to finish as soon as I can."

> **Don't lie, ever.** You can misdirect. You can decline to answer. You can be diplomatic. You can understate. But **never lie** in an interview. It's not necessary (there are true things that you can present in a positive light), plus, you might get caught.

> **Think before you speak.** It's totally OK for there to be a pause between the end of a question and the beginning of your answer. That pause gives you time for reflection, or just to take a breath and pull yourself together.

> **If you don't know something, say so.** You are not required to be the expert on everything in the world, or even in your own life. So if your interviewer asks, "What was your departmental budget on that job you had eight years ago?" it's fine for you to say, "I don't recall, but I can try to find out for you." It's also fine to answer a question that's designed to put you on the spot ("Why haven't you been promoted yet?") by simply saying, "I don't know."

> **Don't put your interviewer to sleep.** While you're answering a question, watch your interviewer closely and try to see if he or she is truly engaged, or is just going through the motions of being polite. Sometimes, this can be hard to tell; but if your interviewer's eyes are looking glazed, or wandering to the clock or the door, take that seriously. Wrap up what you're saying as fast as you can, and keep your next few answers animated or brief. If you've made your main point first, it's much easier to wrap up than it is if you're still leading up to that point!

OK, you've got guidelines, you've got ground rules, and you've got your list of questions.

Next step? Gathering the facts and figures, stories and experiences, that will help you answer whatever questions you're asked.

TRY THIS

Take your lists of Generic, Job-Related, and Awkward questions and put check marks next to the ones that you think can be answered with a simple Statement.

Then go over those lists again and note which questions can be answered with specific details, and which ones are best answered more generally.

TO SUM IT ALL UP...

Most of what you'll do in job interviews is answer questions. Many of them can be answered with simple Statements.

> Your goal in answering every question should be **to demonstrate that you're the person they should hire.**

> Sometimes, to do this, you'll have to guess **what your interviewer really wants to know** ("the question behind the question"), and respond to that underlying concern, which is usually some variation on "Why should we hire you?"

> There are lots of variables in answering questions, but these tips are always relevant:

◆ Answer your interviewer's question first.

◆ Don't lie, ever.

◆ Think before you speak.

◆ If you don't know something, say so.

◆ Don't put your interviewer to sleep.

Chapter 8:

What Happens When You Need to Elaborate?

How to Create Success Stories and Instant Speeches

In Chapter 7, we talked about the fact that, while some generic, job-related, and awkward questions can be answered with a simple Statement, others require a lengthier discussion or story.

Those questions are open-ended, and often begin with a phrase such as:

> ❯ "Tell me about a time when..."
> ❯ "Why do you think that...?"
> ❯ "What would you do if...?"

As soon as you hear a question like that, ask yourself whether what's needed is a **Success Story** about something you've accomplished or learned, or an **Instant Speech** — a format that's useful when you're presenting a particular point of view.

Whichever form you choose, it's not hard to use these formats to your advantage if you prepare and practice them in advance.

Business Stories Have a Beginning, a Middle, and a (Positive) End

If you've ever watched a movie or read a book, you know what a story is. Stories are basically three-part descriptions of an interesting or exciting event:

> ❯ In the first part (the **beginning**), someone's situation changes. Movies often begin with a disaster like a murder, a bridge collapse, or an alien invasion. Business stories begin with a **challenge** (non-business people would call this a *problem*) that could become a disaster if it's not handled properly. The challenge could be anything from an unhappy client to finding contamination in your food processing plant.

> ❯ The **middle** of a story is where people try to fix what went wrong in the beginning. In the alien invasion example, the Avengers assemble and figure out how they're going to save Earth. In a business story, this section includes the **actions taken** to address the challenge. You don't want to include *every* action you took, because that would slow your story way down. But you do need to give enough details to show your listeners that success was not assured.

> ❯ At the **end** of a story, the problem has been resolved (Earth has survived). In a business story, this is called the **outcome**, and it often includes a measure of business success, such as the amount of money you saved. Soft measures like client satisfaction and recommendations count, too.

My Story About George

Challenge: Last month, I got a call from a research biochemist named George. He was about to pitch a project — synthesizing a new, complex molecule — to some high-powered funders, and he didn't have a clue about how to explain his work to non-biochemists.

Actions Taken: George brought a 40-slide PowerPoint to our first consultation. I didn't understand a word of it, so we decided to start from scratch. Over the next few hours, we created a 15-slide deck that was easy for laypeople to follow, used fun images, and explained the "stickiness" of his molecule by comparing it to the gluten in bread.

Outcome: Two weeks later, George called to say that, in spite of some tough competition, his project was going to be fully funded to the tune of $2M. He was thrilled about this, and I was, too.

Keeping Your Story in Balance

Did you notice, in this example, that each section — Challenge, Actions Taken, and Outcome — was roughly the same length?

That's no accident, and the reason for it is simple:

By making your three sections roughly equal in length, you'll avoid the temptation to either load one section up with too much detail, or to skip over the most important parts of another.

You'll also give your story a nice balance and flow.

This isn't the kind of thing you want to worry about when you're telling a story off-the-cuff. But since you'll be preparing your stories in advance, try giving equal time and weight to the beginning (challenge), middle (actions taken), and end (outcome).

(And by the way, I edited that little story about George at least eight times. Streamlining a complicated story so that you can tell it quickly yet clearly takes a lot of trial and error. In fact, if a story sounds "effortless," this *proves* that someone worked hard on it!)

Your Success Stories Are Versatile

Once you've got a good Success Story, it can serve many purposes. Here are just some of the questions that I could answer by telling my story about George:

> "Tell us about a time when you solved a problem in a creative or unexpected way." (George didn't expect me to throw out his PowerPoint, but I knew that would be a better solution.)

> "Do you work well under pressure?" (Yes, I'm fast and focused under pressure. My work with George illustrates this.)

> "You don't have any formal science training. How will you be able to write for our scientists?" (Let me tell you about my client George. If I could translate the biochemistry of *his* project for a lay audience, I can write about your projects, too.)

> "Do you produce results for your clients?" (Yes. One of my clients, a biochemist named George...)

Your stories are also versatile.

Let's say that, last year, you finished a difficult project on time and under budget, even though half your staff had just been laid off.

If that were true, your story about that success could be used to answer these typical interview questions, and many more:

> "Talk about a time that you succeeded against the odds."

> "Do you have experience working with limited resources?"

> "What kind of a leader are you?"

And what if you had a volatile client that nobody thought you'd ever win over, but you did? The story of how you tamed that client could be used to illustrate your persistence, creativity, flexibility, self-confidence, your winning way with difficult people, and many other qualities or skills that would be valuable to the organization that's interviewing you.

Use This Format for Other Stories, Too

Although we're mostly talking about business **Success Stories** (the ones in which you solved a problem or met a challenge), you can also use this approach for telling job interview stories that answer more personal questions.

An example would be, "Why did you decide to become a [your profession or job title]?"

Here's my answer to that question:

Beginning: "When I was a kid, I wanted to be either a writer or a jazz singer. I actually sang for about 18 years, but long-term, it just wasn't working out."

Middle: "So I looked for ways that I could make a living as a writer, and got into corporate speechwriting. I wrote literally hundreds of speeches, began coaching executives to deliver them, and discovered that coaching was my favorite part of the process."

End: "So I started my own speaker coaching business, and now I work with clients from all walks of life who are passionate about speaking well. It's fun, it's interesting, and I love helping my clients succeed."

Just as with my example about George, this story didn't pop into my head fully formed.

I wrote down some ideas and then tweaked them, said them out loud, tweaked them, said them out loud, and went through that process again and again until I had something that flowed and was easy to say.

That's the ideal way to create a story, and we'll talk more about why later.

For now, just know that you *will* be able to create **Success Stories** that **demonstrate why you're the person they should hire.** These stories will address your interviewer's true concerns and put you in the best possible light!

Plus, you'll be able to use those stories to answer not one, but a wide variety of job interview questions!

When You Need To Present a Point of View, Make an Instant Speech

Instant Speech is my name for an easy-to-use format that adds authority and credibility to any discussion or argument.

You would make an instant speech in cases where (a) you want to explain yourself, or (b) you have a point of view that you're trying to communicate.

For instance, what if someone asks you, "You've only been out of college for three years. What makes you think you're qualified to be an IT Director?"

This question invites you to **argue a point**, and you'll need all the credibility and persuasiveness you can muster to counter the interviewer's assumption that you're too young to be a business leader. This is a good time to make an Instant Speech.

How to Create an Instant Speech

It's easy to create an Instant Speech if you follow these three steps *in this order:*

> **Decide on your main point (sometimes called your Key Message).** Notice that this is exactly what you would do if

you were answering a question with a simple Statement. And don't worry about making your main point original, sophisticated, or articulate; the best main points are simple and strong.

> **Now support that point with one, two, or three statements, facts, or examples.** These are called supporting points. Three is an effective number of supporting points (this is called the "Rule of 3" in public speaking circles), but it's OK to use fewer if there aren't three things you want to say about your main point.

> **Then repeat your main point again, as a summary.** This repetition of your main point is the last thing your listener will hear. It will stick in his or her mind, create a sense of closure, and be *the thing that he or she remembers.* You may feel silly making the same point twice, but ignore that qualm. Don't leave it out!

In the example above ("You've only been out of college for three years. What makes you think you're qualified to be an IT Director?"), your Instant Speech might sound like this:

> **Opening Main Point:** "Even though I'm just 25, I'm well-qualified to be an IT Director, for these reasons:"

> **Supporting Points:** "First, I've been working in the industry since I was 16, and have supervised teams of up to 20 people. Second, although my last title was "Supervisor," I was doing Director-level work, as you can see from my resume. And third, I was up for a promotion to Director when my last organization folded."

> **Summary Main Point:** "So for all of those reasons, I believe that I'm more than ready to be an IT Director, and I'd love the chance to prove it to you."

The Softer Side of Instant Speeches

That's a pretty strong argument — and sometimes, a little forcefulness is what it takes to get your point across. But you can also use the Instant Speech format to give weight to what might otherwise come across as a "soft" answer.

For example, if someone asks, "Why do you want to work for our organization?" you could say,

> **Opening Main Point:** "I want to work for your organization because of the chance to grow my engineering skills."

> **Supporting Points:** "In the last five years, you've run major projects on five continents. Each of them has broken new creative ground. And you're known for taking junior engineers onsite and letting them get their hands dirty."

> **Summary Main Point:** "That's an incredible opportunity to learn new engineering skills, and that's why I would love to work for your organization."

This approach works for non-profit organizations, too:

> **Opening Main Point:** "I'd like to work for your organization because I think it would be a great match."

> **Supporting Points:** "I admire the work you do with local human rights groups around the world. I also think that you produce exceptional research about the state of human rights in different countries. And it would be challenging and exciting to work with your team to lobby Congress."

> **Summary Main Point:** "So for me, this would be a perfect match, and that's why I want to work with you."

And it work for service organizations, too (in fact, it works for any situation):

> **Opening Main Point:** "I'd like to work for you because your company treats its drivers well."

> **Supporting Points:** "I appreciate your flexible scheduling. Your fleet is in great condition. And your benefits and salaries are fair."

> **Summary Main Point:** "I think you're the best limo outfit in town, and that's why I'd like to be one of your drivers."

See how the Instant Speech format gives these answers extra weight?

Sure you could have given all those answers as simple Statements, ("I want to work for you because I'll grow my skills... or, you reflect my values... or, you're the best at what you do.") But the Instant Speech format expanded those answers, and gave them extra punch.

That's why it adds to both your confidence and your credibility.

TRY THIS

At the end of the last chapter, you selected the generic, job-related, and awkward questions on your list that could be answered by Statements, and those that seemed to need something more.

Have you changed your mind about any of those questions?

Look at the ones that "needed something more," and see which ones you would answer with a Success Story, and which ones you'd answer using an Instant Speech. (Remember that Success Stories can talk about "unsuccessful" experiences, as long as you learned something in the end.)

TO SUM IT ALL UP...

> Some questions require a longer answer than you can make with a **Statement**. When that's the case, answer them with a **Success Story**, to show something that you accomplished or learned, or an **Instant Speech**, to argue or explain a particular point.

> While stories have a beginning, middle, and end, business **Success Stories** have a **challenge**, a section about the **actions taken** to overcome that challenge, and an **outcome** that should include some "metric," or way of measuring your success.

> **Instant Speeches** start with a straightforward main point, then make one, two, or three supporting points (three is preferable), and end with a repeat of the main point (which now serves as a summary. This is a good way to deliver an explanation or argue for a point of view, particularly if you or your credentials are challenged in the interview.

Chapter 9:
To Know What You've Done, Research Yourself

To answer interview questions well, you're going to need more than some useful formats.

You're going to need actual **information** about what you've accomplished over your career, and the strengths and skills that will make you a great person to hire.

So to get that information, let's launch a treasure hunt — similar to what you did in Chapter 5 — but this time, with *you* as the subject.

"Research Myself?"

Why, you may be wondering, would you bother researching yourself?

Don't you already know about yourself? Don't you remember the significant things you've done in your career?

Well, not necessarily. Just because you lived through something doesn't mean that it's immortalized in your memory. And given how much new stuff comes into our brains every day, the chances are good that you've forgotten important details and even big things that you accomplished just a few years back.

Want to test that? Without looking at your resume, quick, tell me:

> What's the title you had in your second job?;

> What's the largest number of people you've ever worked with on a team, and what did that team accomplish?; and

> Name three positive qualities that you bring to your work.

Some of you will be able to reel off those answers, and for others, the questions won't be relevant (maybe you haven't had a second job yet, or even a first). But most people will stumble over at least one of those questions; and if you're stumbling, or scrambling to think up information, you're not presenting yourself in the best possible light.

Three Categories of You

On the other hand, you can answer almost any question smoothly and successfully if you've gathered some data in these three categories:

> Your **assets** (the skills, strengths, and positive qualities that will make you valuable to an organization);

> **Your successful work experiences** (these will become the basis of your Success Stories); and

> **What you've learned** from the things that didn't go as well as you hoped they would.

Now, as you've probably noticed, I'm fond of organizing things into groups of three. So I would make a list for each of those categories.

But the key here is not whether you make one list or three lists. It's that you **become familiar with the aspects of yourself and your experience that you'll be talking about during your interview.**

The information that you gather in this chapter will become the basis for the Statements, Success Stories, and Instant Speeches that you create; so gather well!

First, List Your Assets

You'd think that functioning adults would know as much about our strengths as we do about our weaknesses, but that's usually not the case. Many people can list where they fall short with little or no effort. But tell them to list their *positive qualities* and they freeze.

Whether it's easy or hard for you to get in touch with the positive characteristics and qualities that make you a desirable employee, sit down and start making that list now.

And remember: You don't have to just think about work when you're making this list. The same qualities that make you a valuable neighbor, friend, parent, etc., also make you valuable at your job.

So scan every area of your life for things to put on the list, including the strengths and skills that you've displayed in:

> School
> Sports
> Hobbies
> Friendships
> Family
> Community
> Religion
> Military service

Can you think of any good things to say about how you've operated in these areas? Are you, perhaps:

> Smart?
> Friendly?

> Conscientious?
> Creative?
> Determined?
> Intuitive?
> Disciplined?
> Forgiving?
> Protective?

Using whatever you take notes with (pen, pencil, tablet, computer, smart phone, etc.), capture **30 of the positive qualities or characteristics** you've demonstrated in *any* area of your life to date.

(And yes, push yourself to really list 30 things. Set an alarm and see if you can do it in five minutes, which means listing one good thing every 10 seconds.)

No Brag, Just Fact

At this point, you may be thinking, "I can't brag about myself. That's totally obnoxious."

Agreed, obnoxious bragging is out. But **it's not bragging when you simply state the facts.** And even though you can't weigh accomplishments, or measure the width of a challenge overcome, these things are matters of "public record." So in my view,

> The things that you've accomplished in your career are **fact.**

> The challenges that you've overcome are **fact.**

> The skills that you bring to the workplace are **fact.**

> And your personal assets — the things that make you valuable, admirable, and/or different from other people — are also fact, though in a more general sense of that word.

As an example, I have a beautiful voice. That's something I've known all my life, and have been told hundreds of times; and I'm confident that "has a beautiful voice" is an asset I possess. Even though it can't be quantified in the way that you could quantify my height, weight, age, etc., it's a matter of public record. It's **fact.**

You also have personal assets that everyone around you agrees on. If you would prefer to call these **widespread opinions** rather than facts, that's fine. But no matter what you call them, be sure to *write them down on your list!*

Still having trouble getting to 30 assets?

Ask a friend or family member — one who knows how to give a compliment — to help you with your list.

You may not be clear about your assets, but chances are good that the people who care about you know just what they are!

List Your Successes at Work

If you never meet your own high expectations, this exercise may also prove challenging. But there's probably a "paper trail" — or, more likely, a series of computer files — to help remind you of what you've accomplished.

Sit down, alone or with a good friend, and take a mental walk through your work history, using old resumes, pay stubs, computer files, and whatever other records you have as an aid to memory.

Starting no more than 10 years ago, review what you accomplished in every job you've held. Did you:

> Work on any big or complicated projects?
> Get promoted?
> Help a team succeed at something important?

> Solve a tough problem?
> Step up and take extra responsibility?
> Receive special recognition?
> Make a difference to the people around you?
> Win big praise from a client?
> Persevere at something difficult?
> Pull off something you weren't sure could be done?

These "above and beyond" experiences of success — along with the "routine" times you met a goal, performed well, created good will, or saved the day — will become the Success Stories that you tell in your job interviews.

Now List Your Job-Related Mistakes, and the Things You Learned From Them

As you learned in Chapter 8, there's no such thing as a Failure Story in business. So on *this* pass through your own "back pages," look for experiences that didn't go well. When you find those experiences, think about what you learned from them. Did you learn to:

> Ask for help sooner rather than later?
> Leave more time for a project than you think you'll need?
> Let your direct reports have more freedom to do their work in the way they think best (or conversely, keep a closer watch on their progress)?
> Refrain from gossiping?
> Document the progress of a job?
> Double-check your client's expectations?
> Triple-check your operating budget?

There's always something new to learn from our own mistakes, and being able to speak about what you've learned turns failure into success, and shows an openness and humility on your part.

And now that you've reviewed your assets, successes, and lessons learned, you're ready to turn your self-research into Statements, Success Stories, and Instant Speeches in Chapter 10.

TRY THIS

Were you surprised by some of the positive things that came to light when you researched yourself?

If so, talk to a friend or spend some quiet time thinking about the accomplishments you've just rediscovered.

In the same way that *becoming your Avatar* will help you deal with interview-related fear, reviewing your own strengths, skills, accomplishments, and lessons learned will remind you that **you're the person they should hire!**

TO SUM IT ALL UP...

> Although most people can easily recall their faults, many of us forget or overlook our accomplishments. That's why it's important to "research yourself" to uncover the positives about who you are, and what you've done.

> To find your **assets**, the positive qualities and characteristics that will make you a great employee, review every area of your life, not just the jobs you've held.

> Also list your **successes**, and **what you learned** when things didn't go according to plan.

> If making these lists is difficult, ask a trusted person to help you. And remember, while you never want to sound arrogant or obnoxious, you're not bragging if what you say is a matter of public record ("fact").

Chapter 10:

How to Connect Who You Are and What You've Done to the Questions You're Being Asked

You've made up questions, thought about questions, made lists that will help you with your questions, and now you're going to... answer questions.

The goal here is two-fold: You're going to come up with **real, live answers** that you can use in **real, live interviews.** But you'll also learn *an approach to answering questions* that will serve you well when you get asked a question you didn't anticipate.

First, Get Your Tools Ready

To make this happen, you'll need the following materials:

> Your list(s) of **assets, successes,** and **lessons learned**

> Your list(s) of **generic questions, job-related questions,** and **awkward questions**

> **Whatever you use to write or record with** (pen, pencil, tablet, computer, smart-phone, voice recorder, etc.)

> If you've been **working with someone** — a coach, an advisor, or a friend — you'll probably want them to join you for this exercise, too.

OK, ready?

Prepare an Answer that's a Statement

Let's walk through this process together, using the sample question, *"Why do you want to work for this organization?"*

Like many other interview questions, this one could be answered with either a Statement or an Instant Speech. Fortunately, you don't have to choose at this point — because **the Statement that you prepare can either stand alone or become the main point of an Instant Speech** if you decide you want to add more detail.

So for now, focus on the Statement answer, and let's do each of the following steps:

> **Get into your Avatar.** Before doing this exercise, make sure you've got your game face on. (And if you haven't been practicing being your best self, now is the time to begin!)

> **Read the question out loud.** It's important for you to hear the question, because you'll be hearing (not reading) it during the interview. So you or your practice partner should actually speak the question, "Why do you want to work for this organization?"

> Now just to get the ball rolling, **ANSWER THE QUESTION WITHOUT CENSORING YOURSELF.** In other words, say what's really in your heart or on your mind; for example, "Are you kidding me? At this point, I'll take any job I can get!" The reason to get your uncensored response out in the open is that, if you do this, you're less likely to trip over these thoughts or feelings later.

> **Check for a "question behind the question."** This question seems pretty straightforward, so you can answer it as asked. But don't forget that your goal is to **demonstrate that you're the person they should hire**, by satisfying your interviewer's concern while putting yourself in the best possible light.

> **Time to strategize.** Because this question is about the *organization*, take a quick look at your research about them. Is there something about this organization that you find genuinely interesting or admirable? If so, make that the reason you give in your answer. If not, choose something that *the organization* wants to be admired for.

> **Make a simple, clear Statement** that answers the question and gives the reason you've chosen. For example: "I'd like to work here because I admire your organization's culture," or "I want to use my research skills in a company that provides room to grow," or "I want to join your group because I believe in your products and would like to sell them."

> **Write down your answer.** If you haven't written down your answer, do it now. Seeing the answer in writing will give you a different perspective on it, and help you remember what you've decided to say.

> **Double-check yourself.** Is your answer respectful of the organization? Make sure you haven't said the equivalent of, "I'd love to work for you because you're only 10 minutes from my apartment," or "With my work history, this is probably the best I can do."

> **Practice delivering your answer.** Pretend that you're at the interview, and have someone ask you the practice question. Now answer it as your Avatar would, while feeling your positive "best self" qualities.

> **Keep practicing your answer.** Deliver your answer 2, 3, 4, 5 times, while being your best self. But don't answer with exactly the same words each time. Instead, every time you practice, make small changes in your words, or in how you say them, so you don't get stale or start sounding "canned." Try to feel more relaxed, comfortable and confident with every repetition.

> While you practice, you may find a better answer, or a better way of stating your idea. If you do, update your

written answer to reflect those changes. **But don't make changes unless they're really better** ("If it ain't broke, don't fix it!"), and don't spend time editing your answer on paper instead of practicing it out loud.

This may sound like a lot of steps to take, but most of them go by very quickly.

And one important note: If someone is helping you with this exercise, make sure they understand that your GOAL is to **demonstrate why this organization should hire you** by addressing the interviewer's concerns while putting yourself in the best possible light. Do *not* let your practice partner pressure you to quote from your resume, "pad" your statements by adding non-essential details, or overtly pitch yourself ("You should hire me because I'll be the best ER nurse you've ever seen").

Stick with the program, and ask your partner to do the same.

Statement Answers to Awkward Questions

It's pretty easy to come up with simple Statements in answer to "softball" questions.

But when it comes to questions that freeze your brain and strike fear in your heart — and everyone has at least one of those — things can seem a lot harder.

As we've discussed, these questions might include zingers like:

> ❯ "There are some breaks in your employment history. What were you doing during those periods?"
> ❯ "Why did you leave your last position?"
> ❯ "Why did you drop out of college?"
> ❯ "Why do you think you haven't been promoted beyond the junior manager level?"

Notice all those "why"s? The word makes many people defensive even when that's not the questioner's intention.

The steps that you used to answer easier questions will also work for answering these — but **first, you need to get your brain unfrozen!**

Here are two techniques that can help:

> Give yourself a quick **attitude adjustment**. Push away any guilt, embarrassment, or awkwardness the question inspires. Remember: Nobody is perfect, and nobody has a perfect job history, let alone a history of constant success. How well do you think *the person who's interviewing you* would do if you put their work history under a microscope?

> If you have any doubts about the correct **strategy** to use in answering these questions, get advice from anyone who's given you good career help in the past, whether that's your practice partner, spouse, colleague, mentor, friend, or coach. Someone else can often see an easy approach to answering a question that has you totally flummoxed.

Also, don't forget that **while you want to give a truthful answer, you are not required to tell "the truth, the whole truth, and nothing but the truth"!**

Here are some examples of tactful answers to awkward questions, along with how the answers would sound if they were the truth, the whole truth, and nothing but the truth. (And if these questions don't seem awkward to you, remember that awkwardness is completely subjective; one person's humiliating moment can be another person's total shrug.)

Question: Have you done much exhibition design?

Answer: I've done some, and I'm looking forward to doing a lot more. Will that be an important part of the job?
[The full truth: I've done very little exhibition design]

Question: Why did you relocate to New York?

Answer: I've always dreamed of living here, so I asked my old organization for a transfer.
[The full truth: Also, I was getting a divorce.]

Question: How are you at taking direction?

Answer: I take direction well.
[The full truth: I *can* take direction well. But if my manager is an idiot, I'll probably just ignore him and do what I think is best for the team.]

You get the picture. A lot of tact and a little forethought can save you from those awkward moments when the interviewer asks a question and the only thing you can think of to do or say is crawl under the desk, or scream.

Turning Your Statement into an Instant Speech

In Chapter 8, we talked about the Instant Speech format, and how it can make an explanation, or argument sound more authoritative. The Instant Speech format does this by starting **and ending** with a main point that is remarkably similar to the Statement answers you just created.

Let's look at how that works:

Question: "Why do you want to work for this organization?"

> ❯ To answer this question, start with your **Statement**: "I'd like to work here because I admire your organization's culture."

Now, you could leave it at that, and be fine.

But let's say that you've thought a lot about the organization's culture, and want to add more. In that case, just treat your Statement like an Opening Main Point, and go on to add three supporting points.

> **Supporting Points:** "I saw on your web site that every employee does community service, which I think is great. And you also talk about developing your people and promoting from within. Plus it sounds like a place where people actually like each other."

Now wrap it up with a repeat of your Main Point. It's OK to vary how you state this point, but be sure that *the point itself remains the same* as what you opened with:

> **Summary Main Point:** Those are all things that matter to me, and I'd love to work in an organization with that kind of culture.

See how that works? Let's take one of the answers to awkward questions above, and do the same thing:

Question: "Why did you relocate to New York?"

> **Statement / Opening Main Point:** "I've always dreamed of living here, so I asked my old organization for a transfer."

> **Supporting Points:** "At first, they were reluctant, but I really wanted to do this. So finally, they gave me the transfer, and I moved here fourteen months ago. But, of course, what I didn't realize was that they were going to close their New York office a year later."

> **Summary Main Point:** "So, yeah, I always dreamed of living here, but things haven't gone quite the way I planned."

These two examples, along with the examples in Chapter 8 should give you a clear picture of how Instant Speeches work. But if you want more examples, or more detailed instruction, check out Chapters 4 through 6 in my first book, *Speak Like Yourself... No, Really! Follow Your Strengths and Skills to Great Public Speaking.*

And remember: This kind of skill can only be learned by *doing!* So now that you've read two examples of how to turn a Statement into an Instant Speech, go ahead and try it using Statements that *you've* created.

When Instant Speeches and Success Stories Overlap

As you know from Chapter 8, the difference between **Instant Speeches** and **Success Stories** is that Success Stories have a beginning (challenge), a middle (actions taken), and an end (outcome), whereas Instant Speeches have **supporting points** that add weight to your main point.

But sometimes, when you're making an Instant Speech, your three supporting points will drift into a Success Story, as they began to do in the "Why did you relocate to New York?" answer above.

If that happens, go with it! Don't get hung up on repeating your main point; instead, give your story a strong ending that gives your listener a sense of closure, like this:

Question: "Why did you relocate to New York?"

> **Statement / Opening Main Point:** "I've always dreamed of living here, so I asked my old organization for a transfer."

> **Supporting Points that Drift Into Being the Action Section of a Success Story:** "At first, they were reluctant, but I really wanted to do this. So finally, they gave me the transfer, and I moved here fourteen months ago. It was hard to adjust, but I did. I started feeling like a New Yorker right about the time that my company closed their New York office.

> **Success Story Outcome:** "Which is why I'm looking for a new job. Half of my dream of living in New York has come true, and now I'm looking to fulfill the other half, which is to find a job that I love."

As you can see, **these formats can be applied flexibly. They're meant to help you, not to lock you into speaking in a particular way.** So take what you learn from this book as a guide, but don't ignore your own instincts and judgment.

And if you find yourself suddenly telling a story, **tell the story** — don't worry about the format!

Choosing Statements, Success Stories, or Instant Speeches

OK, it's your turn.

You're now going to take several of your own Statement answers and turn them into either **Success Stories, Instant Speeches**, or both.

Since there's such a large area of overlap between Statements, Success Stories, and Instant Speeches, how do you know which ones to use when? You practiced making this decision in the TRY THIS section of Chapter 8, but here's a method you can use when you're asked a new question and have to choose an approach on the fly:

› Open-ended questions that ask you to **describe something** may make good **Success Stories**. We'll look at how to deal with those in a minute.

› As you know, **Instant Speeches** are ideal for arguing a point. They're also great when you have several things you want to say, because those things can become Supporting Points.

› And questions that don't obviously fall into either of those categories can probably be answered with simple **Statements**. Since a Statement can easily evolve into a Success Story or Instant Speech in mid-stream, you can never go wrong using it as your starting point.

In fact, as you've just seen, you can always change your mind about what approach to use with each question. But one caution: **base any mid-answer changes to your game plan on your *interviewer's* reaction, not on *your own* momentary twinges of doubt.**

If your *interviewer* seems intrigued, say more. If he or she looks like they've already got your point and is ready to ask another question, wrap it up.

In either case, you'll be prepared to adjust because of the thinking and practicing you've done in advance.

Sketching Out Your Success Stories

The process to follow when you create a Success Story is, not surprisingly, very similar to the Instant Speech process.

Let's say that you're preparing an answer to the question, ***"Tell me about a time when you went above and beyond for your team":***

> First, get into your **Avatar.**

> Read the question **out loud.**

> ANSWER THE QUESTION **WITHOUT CENSORING YOURSELF.**

> **Check for a "question behind the question."** In this case, they seem to want an example of the kind of employee you will be. So a story about the time your team was working late and you treated everyone to pizza won't satisfy their *real* concern.

> **Time to strategize.** This question is about you, so look at your research notes from Chapter 9 for a team situation in which you took leadership or fulfilled your usual role in a way that went "above and beyond."

> **Explain the "Challenge" (beginning) in a clear and brief way.** This is good time to remind yourself that *your goal is not to paint a comprehensive picture* of the challenge you faced and the myriad details that led up to it. Your GOAL is to *demonstrate that you're the person they should hire* by answering the interviewer's concerns while putting yourself in the best possible light.

> **Define the "Outcome" (what happened at the end of your efforts).** Yes, since you have the luxury of planning this story in advance, we are skipping over the middle section for now. (If you were telling the story in real time, the "middle section would come next.

>> ◆ Why? Because **the *outcome* of your story determines which details you'll share in the middle section.** If my outcome is that *the team was happy,* the middle section of my story will focus more on my interactions with team members and less on my negotiations with the Finance Department. If my outcome is that *we saved money,* it will be the reverse.

>> ◆ If you don't have specific measures of success (metric) to use as an outcome, try to **be as specific as possible about the benefit your actions helped create for the organization, and how those benefits were recognized.** In other words, if you know this is true, say, "The organization saved almost $200,000 and my manager wrote a commendation for my file." But even if you don't know *how much* the organization saved, it's still an important outcome, so say, "The organization saved money, and my manager wrote a commendation for my file."

> **Now that you know where your story is going, fill in the middle with the "Actions Taken" that turned your challenge into a success.** Again, remember that the goal is not comprehensiveness; it's to show your interviewer what kind of an employee you would be. And if this is a story about what you learned from a "failure," be sure that the Actions Taken clearly show how hard, diligently, creatively, etc. you tried to succeed.

> **Capture phrases or words to jog your memory.** It's not helpful to write down a story in the early stages of developing it — you want to refine your story by hearing it *out loud*, not by reading it on paper. But do write down a few key words that will help you remember what you've said, particularly in the versions you like best.

> **Practice delivering your story.** Get into your Avatar, pretend you're at the interview, and tell your story out loud, preferably to someone who will *not* say, "You left out mentioning the fourth time we asked our client to give us his decision." What you're looking for as you keep practicing is simplicity, clarity, and a sense that you've made your point, not comprehensiveness. Remember your GOAL!

> **Keep practicing and refining your story.** My stories don't usually fall into place until I've delivered them about ten times. So take your time, play with the story, and feel free to try adding or taking away details or changing how you say something.

> When you like the way your story is flowing, **update your notes** so that you'll remember this version. Then **keep practicing it regularly.** You're better off telling your story once a day for a week than you would be if you ignored it for a week and then practiced for an hour.

> Finally, remember the discussion in Chapter 6 about how many questions can be answered with the same story? **Make a list of other questions your story could answer.** This step will help you get more benefit from your stories and the time that you invest in them.

Putting the Success Story Process to Work

Here is a story of mine that could be used to answer the question **"Tell me about a time when you went above and beyond for your team."** (It could also be used to answer questions like: "What is your management style?" "How would you describe your work ethic?" "Tell me about a time when you accomplished something you didn't think was possible," and more.)

I started my thought process about this question by coming up with an **"Above and Beyond" Statement** that quickly summed up my answer, "I once had to literally do the work of three writers to get a big job done on time."

Then, with that answer in mind, I developed a Success Story that makes the same point but with lots more information about how I operate in work situations:

As you read this story, see if you can spot the beginning and end of the Challenge, Actions Taken, and Outcome sections. And notice that **the highlighted phrases and sentences create a shorter version of the story** that I could tell if time was tight, or my interviewer seemed less interested.

"Above and Beyond" Story:

"Before starting my own speaker coaching business, I was involved in a year-long project where I supervised two other writers. Things were fine at the beginning, but gradually, these writers started spending more time complaining and less time working. They complained about their pay, their working conditions, their assignments, our clients, everything. They were hurting everyone's morale, and **finally the person in charge of that project decided, with my agreement, to let them go.**

"Of course, we both figured that we would just go out and find new writers to pick up where our two complainers left off. But because it was a specialized industry, and because of the short time frame before the project was finished, we just couldn't find the talent we needed.

"What quickly became clear was that I was going to have to pick up the slack. **I ended up** working almost around the clock for several months. I was **doing the work of three people,** but at least I knew it was getting done right, **and I learned a lot about what it takes to perform under extreme stress.**

"**The project was a major success.** It was touch-and-go toward the very end, but I don't think our clients ever realized we were down two writers. They were thrilled, and my boss gave me a generous bonus. **So it turned out to be a great experience, even though I wouldn't want to do it again."**

TRY THIS

Choose one of *your* successes and describe what you accomplished in a simple Statement.

Then sketch out a more detailed Success Story that answers an interviewer's concerns about how you react to unusual demands, and that puts your best self forward.

TO SUM IT ALL UP...

Before you start answering the generic, job-related, and awkward questions you've listed, **gather all your research materials.**

> You've already identified questions that you think can be answered with simple Statements. **Answer those first,** using the process outlined in this Chapter.

> Now **turn some of those Statements into Instant Speeches, and others into Success Stories.**

> **Create other Success Stories and Instant Speeches from scratch,** beginning with your Challenge (for Success Stories) or Opening Main Point (for Instant Speeches).

> For each answer that you've created, **note some *other* questions** you could use it to answer.

> Practice **delivering** the answers you've created **out loud**, over and over, until you can deliver them with confidence and ease.

> **Throughout this preparation and practice**, be sure to (a) stay in your Avatar; (b) stay flexible; and (c) keep your eye on the GOAL of **demonstrating that you're the right person for them to hire** by satisfying your interviewer's concerns while putting yourself in the best possible light.

Chapter 11:
How to Practice for Success

Up until now, you've been preparing and practicing **what** you're going to say at your next job interview.

Now it's time to give a little attention to **how** you're going to say it.

And by the way, if you *haven't* been preparing and practicing, do yourself a favor and start today! Even if you don't have an interview lined up, preparing for the interview you hope or expect to get soon will put you ahead of the game and make you less likely to panic when that interview gets booked.

Plus, **public speaking practice never goes to waste.** The skills you're developing throughout this book will serve you not just in job interviews but in conferences, meetings, pitches, briefings, networking events, and even in conversations with your friends and family.

But practicing doesn't just mean saying words out loud. As you'll see, it includes practicing your *attitude*.

Here are my suggestions for ***what to practice***, and why:

Practice Feeling Relaxed, Confident, Competent, and Friendly

Whether or not those qualities are built into your Avatar, they will serve you well as you practice for job interviews.

> **Why practice being relaxed?** Remember that an interview is a *conversation*, not a *test*. So put yourself in a relaxed, conversational frame of mind **whenever you are thinking about, working on, or practicing for an interview.**

> **Why practice a confident awareness of your own competence?** Because people will believe what you tell them about yourself! If you present yourself as insecure and incompetent (through your words, your posture, or lack of eye contact), your interviewer will believe that this is true. So review the skills and strengths that you uncovered in Chapters 3 and 9, and — if you don't feel confident and competent — practice **faking it till you make it.**

> **Why practice feeling friendly toward your interviewer?** Because, as we've discussed before, people are often favorably inclined toward other people who *seem to like them.* If you interviewer has screened two equally qualified candidates, will he or she tilt towards the one who reached out in a friendly and interested way? Or the one who was cold, aloof, or superior?

Practice Your Answers to Questions OUT LOUD

DO NOT make the mistake of thinking that your job is done once you've figured out, or even written down, answers to the generic, job-related, and awkward questions on your lists.

Since **talking to someone** is a very different activity than thinking about or writing down answers, you won't know how well your answers truly work until you've **spoken them out loud, many times.**

Listen to how your answers sound, and make whatever adjustments you need so that they flow more smoothly and comfortably for you.

And whatever you do, don't always say the exact same words in the exact same way when you practice. That kind of practicing can make you sound stiff and artificial, not like someone who's enjoying a lively conversation. To that end, stick with the APPROACH to each question you've decided works best, but vary your words and your delivery a little every time you practice answering a question.

Practice Your Answers Out Loud a LOT

Even after you've crafted your Statements, Success Stories, and Instant Speeches, **delivering them in a relaxed and confident way** takes practice.

If you like practicing with other people, ask several different friends to listen and tell you whether your answers are clear, interesting and not overly long. (Have them take notes while you're talking so that they can give you very specific feedback about things that they liked and where, if anywhere, they were less interested.)

If you prefer to practice alone, record your answers. Most cell phones today can be used as voice recorders; and if you have an old-school answering machine at home, you can call yourself up, give your answer, then listen and do the same analysis.

Most of all, keep remembering that **your goal is not to give a comprehensive report**, but to connect with your interviewer and share something that **demonstrates why you're the person they should hire.**

Practice Being Easily Heard and Understood

Throughout this book, I've encouraged you to make the interviewer's job easier by:

> Trying to anticipate what's really on his or her mind;
> Answering questions in a way that addresses those underlying concerns; and

> Gauging how much or how little you speak based on how your interviewer reacts (the "Don't Bore Your Interviewer" rule).

That's a lot of work on your part, and now I'm going to add to it by asking you to **make it easy for your interviewer to hear you.**

If you've spent much of your adult life communicating by email, text, social media, and cell phone, you may never have thought about being **audibile**, or consciously trying to make yourself easier to hear.

But think for a minute about the poor interviewer who spends his or her day listening to job candidates who:

> Speak at what feels like 500 words a minute; or

> Never stop talking to come up for air; or

> Whisper, mumble, slur, and drop words.

As you can imagine, making yourself easy to hear will help you win this interviewer's heart.

Here are some techniques that can help you:

Open Your Mouth When You Speak

Most of us are lazy talkers.

We sort of halfway open our mouths, and whatever sound falls out of them is good enough for us. After all, if our friends or family members can't hear us, they'll just ask us to repeat what we said, right?

But a job interviewer **may not** ask you to repeat what you just said. Why should they, when they can just cross you off their list of prospective hires?

To make sure that doesn't happen, **open your mouth when you speak.** By opening your mouth, you'll ensure that the sound of your voice can get out of your mouth and into the room, where your interviewer can hear it. If you tend to be a close-mouthed talker, take about thirty seconds each day and practice opening your mouth a bit more as you speak out loud in front of a mirror.

For inspiration, watch a singing show on TV or YouTube. There's a reason why Beyoncé's mouth is open when she sings!

Put Some Energy Into Your Consonants

The second way to be easier to hear is to **pronounce your consonants more vigorously.**

What are consonants? Well, our alphabet divides into two kinds of letters: vowels (A, E, I, O, U, and sometimes Y) and everything else.

Everything else is — you guessed it — consonants. But not all consonants are created equal. Some of them, like "M," are pretty gentle. (Test this by saying "Mmmmmmm" out loud. You won't be getting much bite from that letter.)

And what about other consonants? Some of them — B, J, K, and others — will pop if you put more energy into saying them.

To try this out, take some words that have those letters and try saying them (a) with no special effort; and then (b) with more energy, while listening for the consonants:

bike — BiKe
take — TaKe
job — JoB
joke—JoKe

Sounds different, doesn't it. Again, a few seconds of practice each day will change the way you "ar-TiC-u-laTe" your consonants, and gradually make you much easier to hear.

Here's another trick that you can practice to become more audible:

Emphasize Important Words

Another way to organize what your interviewer is hearing is to emphasize the more important words you're speaking.

Two sentences can have the exact same words, but land very differently on a listener's ear based on which words are emphasized; for example:

♦ "I KNEW it would be a big success." (See? I *knew* it!
♦ "I knew it would be a BIG SUCCESS." (See? It was *successful!*)

Again, **this is not the sort of thing you want to think about while you're in an interview.** But giving it a little advance thought — and practicing occasionally on your family or friends — will point you in the direction of creating more emphasis when you speak during an interview.

Just remember: It's IMPORTANT for an interviewer to HEAR you, and to UNDERSTAND what you're saying. Otherwise, all the time you've spent preparing and practicing to answer questions may not result in the great impression you want to create.

And finally...

Practice The Public Speaking Pause that Refreshes

Yes, that's an advertising slogan. But there *is* a public speaking pause that refreshes, and that pause is the beat of silence that follows the end of an important thought.

(pause)

See how even those micro-seconds of break time you took while you were reading the word "pause" made it easier for you to absorb what I said before it?

(pause)

Not everything that you say at an interview needs to be delineated (separated from what's around it) by silence. But the important ideas do, such as:

"I'd love to work for your organization."

(pause)

"I'm proud of my record of success."

(pause)

"I have the skills that you're looking for."

(pause)

You get the picture. **If it's important, pause to let it sink in.**

And if you put some pauses into your practicing now, they'll come naturally during an interview, when the adrenaline that's likely to be coursing through your veins might otherwise push you to speak too long or too fast.

TRY THIS

It's hard to have fun with public speaking when you're worried about landing a job. But the more fun you have exploring the public speaking techniques in this chapter, the more you'll discover, learn, and retain.

So think about how you can encourage yourself to **play a little with public speaking every day.** Can you use a timer to make sure you give it a few minutes? Practice in the shower? Teach these techniques to your two-year-old? Find a practice partner and compete? Incorporate it into a game of Beer Pong?

Whatever approach works for you is good. Just do your best to enjoy exploring how things change when you pause after ideas... articulate your consonants... open your mouth more... and EMPHASIZE important words.

(Or is that emphasize important WORDS????)

TO SUM IT ALL UP...

No matter how good your answers to interview questions, they won't create the desired effect if the interviewer can't *hear* what you're saying.

> To that end, **add a few minutes of public speaking practice to your daily routine**, and try to make it fun for yourself.

> **Practice public speaking skills** such as:

◆ Opening your mouth when you speak;

◆ Putting more energy into how you pronounce your consonants (particularly the "plosives" like B, J, and K;

◆ Leaving a little pause after every important idea; and

◆ Emphasizing (landing just a little harder on) the words that you think should stand out for your listener.

❯ **Don't work on, or even think about, this stuff in an actual interview.** Instead, make it part of your preparation and practice, so that when you get to the interview, you can just...

Well, that's the topic of Section 3.

Section 3:

Get the JOB!

In Section 1, you **got ready** for the job interview process.

In Section 2, you learned how to **prepare and practice for interviews.**

Now we're going to talk about **what actually happens on Interview Day.**

We'll start with the first impression you make when you walk into the room, and then cover how to establish and build a positive relationship with the interviewer while you're answering his or her questions.

This section also deals with phone and Skype interviews, and will show you how to write the critically-important thank you note that may help seal the deal after your interview.

Chapter 12:
That Big First Impression

After days or even weeks of preparation, you've got an interview tomorrow!

You don't want to walk into it feeling self-conscious because of what you're wearing, or kicking yourself because you forgot to bring extra copies of your resume. So **the night before your interview:**

> **Adjust your attitude.** With your Avatar firmly in place, imagine how competent and confident you're going to feel at tomorrow's interview while you breathe slowly and smile.

> **Practice *lightly*.** Do a little practicing out loud to refresh your memory and get back in touch with the points you want to make. ***But don't cram.*** Staying up all night to study as if your interview is going to be an exam will send yourself the wrong message.

> **Lay out what you're going to wear, and pack anything you want to bring.** This should include:

- A pen and notepad, if you use them;
- A card and stamp, for the thank you note you'll write after the interview (we'll cover that in Chapter 15);
- ***Directions to the appointment*** and a contact phone number in case you're unavoidably delayed;
- A book, music, or a game to help you relax on the way or while you're waiting in the reception room;
- Your notes about the organization;
- ***Your list of questions;***
- Emergency items that might come in handy, such as tissues, cough drops, breath mints, and a snack.

And of course,

◆ *Your business cards and extra copies of your resume.*

> **Try to get some sleep.** And if that doesn't work, at least try to relax and do something enjoyable instead of lying in bed obsessing about the interview. But be very careful about using sleep aids; you'll be better off feeling tired than groggy in the morning.

On **the day itself:**

> **Eat a good breakfast.** This is no time to make your body run on nervous energy; you need fuel! Also drink some water, and carry a bottle of it with you.

> **Gear up your Avatar.** Put on your Avatar before leaving home, for added confidence along the way. Your Avatar has an important role to play today, so don't leave home without him or her.

All of this will help reduce the stress of getting to the interview, so that you can focus on the interview, and not on peripheral things.

What Is "Appropriate" Interview Dress?

Dressing for an interview can be a balancing act. You want to feel comfortable, and feel like yourself, but you also want to show professionalism and respect for the organization and its culture.

The solution is to look **appropriate.** But beyond the obvious (don't wear pajamas), what does that word actually mean?

Well, it turns out to mean several things, depending on the type of organization you're interviewing with — and of course, the year. The tips in this chapter will guide you through three typical office environments of 2014.

And if you're interviewing for non-office positions like construction supervisor, bar manager, or kindergarten teacher, *use the research tips in Chapter 5 to figure out how people dress on the job, and when they're being interviewed for that job.*

"Old School" (Mainstream) Corporate Interviews

It's still 1985 in many corporations. So if you're interviewing with an old, established firm or organization, think conservative. In these environments, your appearance should proclaim your success without calling attention to itself.

Mainstream Hair

> Men, wear it short and neat.

> Women, keep it tamed, whether you do this with an up style (such as a French twist), with barrettes, or with a short (but not too short!) haircut. And of course, keep your hair color mainstream.

> Conservative workplaces tend to frown on "ethnic" styles. If you have dreadlocks or extensions, twist them up or pull them back. Keep your Afro or Jew-fro short. Men, avoid fades or designs.

> If you use hair grooming products, use them sparingly, and make sure they don't have an overwhelming smell. Your hair should look and smell clean.

Mainstream Shoes

> Men, stick to dress shoes in conservative colors (black, brown, navy); and don't forego the spit and polish.

> Women, you can never go wrong with pumps, but watch out for heel heights over 3 inches.

Mainstream Adornment

> Men, stick with a ring, a watch, cufflinks, and/or tie clips. No chains!

> Women, keep your jewelry small, simple, and of good quality. Save the costume jewelry for after you're hired.

> Visible tats or piercings? Except for pierced ears, don't even think about it!

Mainstream Clothing

> Men, make sure your clothing is of good quality and fits you well, and keep every button on your shirt buttoned.

> Women, cleavage and very short skirts aren't "corporate." And make sure your clothes aren't too tight; this isn't what you want people to remember about your interview.

> For both men and women, pastels and classic colors are your best bet. Go easy on the patterns, and make sure that *something* you're wearing is conservatively cut.

Mainstream Make-Up

> Men, none!

> Women, keep it light, and only wear make-up in neutral or classic colors. No black nail polish, white lipstick, or glitter eyes.

Mainstream Scents

> No heavy aftershaves or perfumes. Some people love them, some people hate them. Why take the chance?

> Be sure you smell fresh. If you sweat easily, or are interviewing on a hot day, bring a washcloth, wipes, or even clean clothes so that you can freshen up when you arrive.

What's Appropriate for Interviewing at a Relaxed or Creative Organization?

These guidelines are for many non-profits and companies in fields like IT, social media, film, PR, or event production that have relaxed (though hard-working) cultures:

Relaxed Hair

> Neat, clean, and not distracting. If they compliment your hair, that's good. If they can't think of anything except your hair, not so much.

Relaxed Shoes

> Men, you get lots of leeway here. But before you choose sandals, think: Do you really want to show off your feet?

> Women, I know that some of you are going to wear 5-inch heels no matter what I say; but if you do, at least bring some comfortable flats to wear afterwards.

Relaxed Adornment

> The relaxed audience is the best of all possible worlds when it comes to personal adornment, but go easy! As with your hairstyle, It's great if your interviewer thinks that you look interesting, but your appearance shouldn't become the focal point of your interview.

Relaxed Clothing

> Start with a "Casual Friday" approach (khakis, knit tops, casual but good-quality shoes), then spice things up a *little*. Items like torn clothes, safety pins through your ears, push-up bras with see-through blouses, and muscle man t-shirts are going way too far!

Relaxed Make-Up

> Men, still none unless the organization is very advanced.

> Women, stay well on this side of "The Girl With the Dragon Tattoo." Dramatic is fine; goth or punk aren't until you've got the job and have proven yourself.

Relaxed Scents

> The same as for Mainstream.

Hyper-Casual Workplace? There's Still Such a Thing as "Appropriate"

Strangely, a hyper-casual workplace can be governed by a dress code that's just as strict as the Mainstream or Relaxed codes. If everyone is wearing flip-flops, cargo shorts, or spiky hair, that's a dress code and you should probably wear a cleaned-up version of the same thing for your interview.

Since this one is hard to gauge in advance, try to find an informant within the organization — a receptionist, an admin, an HR person, a friend of a friend — who you can casually ask what people wear to interview at their company.

And whatever that informant says, don't go too crazy!

Whether you're interviewing with a Corporate, Relaxed, or Hyper-Casual organization, **try to dress in a way that will make you and your interviewer comfortable** by choosing clothes and accessories that you can wear with ease, and that fall within the organization's culture.

Your First Impression — Assessing Your Interviewer

One of the first decisions you'll make when you walk into an interview is who you think you're dealing with.

Your guess about what makes this person tick will guide you through the important interaction that follows. So from the moment when you first walk through the door, tune your senses to the impressions that your interviewer delivers.

Start by **seeing** some obvious things. Is the interviewer:

> Male or female?
> Young or older?
> Confident or awkward?
> Attractive or unappealing?
> Warm and welcoming, or formal and stiff? (These attitudes are revealed by posture and facial expression.)
> Private (no personal objects in sight), or someone who shares their interests (through photos, knick-knacks, memorabilia, art work)?

Now tune up your **ears.** Does your interviewer sound like someone who:

> Is educated (a diploma on the walls will also confirm this)?
> Is confident (do they speak firmly and fluently)?
> Comes from the same region as you (are your accents the same)?
> Is enthusiastic and energetic, or just going through the motions?

You can also use your sense of **touch** to get clues:

> Is his or her handshake crushing, or limp, or just right?
> Does it convey authority and confidence? Warmth? Welcome?

None of these observations will make or break your interview, but any or all of them can help you in two ways:

First, it's useful, in the first few minutes that you walk into the room, to **think about something besides how nervous you are.** Focusing your attention on the "audience" rather than yourself is a trick that seasoned public speakers use to their advantage, and you can do the same at this interview.

And second, **observing your interviewer as an actual person** rather than a guard standing at the door of opportunity **will make it easier for you to have a real conversation** with him or her — and that's the best interview strategy of them all!

Their First Impression — Be Relaxed and Likable

You're well prepared for this interview, and you've taken a quick first impression of the person you'll be talking to for the next half hour or so.

Of course, as you do this, he or she is also getting a first-level reading of you. So what would you like that first impression to be?

My advice is that, without being phony or overdoing this, you go for being **likable.**

Likability is an under-rated (or at least under-acknowledged) quality. While it rarely appears on lists of the top characteristics for success, most of us will freely admit that we're drawn to "likable" people — in other words, people we think are attractive... who share our interests... and who seem to be interested in us.

Well, interviewers are no different.

They are also drawn to people who show one or more of these qualities:

> **Attractiveness** — In this context, attractiveness doesn't mean that you're beautiful or sport a six-pack. It means that you do basic things to make yourself appealing. These include (but aren't limited to) being well-groomed, smiling when you're introduced, and maintaining a pleasant and professional demeanor.

> **Share Common Interests** — Here's where your organization and interviewer research comes in. While going through the steps in Chapter 5, you may have discovered some things that you have in common with your interviewer. You may share a hobby, a previous employer, even an *alma mater*.

If you find a strong common interest, try mentioning it at the start of an interview ("I noticed on your organization profile that you grew up in the same town I did."). If your interviewer picks up on this cue ("Really? I haven't been back there in 20 years!"), you have an instant common interest. If he or she just nods or says, "That's nice," just drop the topic; no harm done.

You may also discover a common interest in your interviewer's work space. As you enter, take a quick look at pictures on the desk, diplomas on the wall, even the view out their window — and don't be afraid to comment on what you see.

> **Show Interest in Your Interviewer**—Whether or not you find something to chat with your interviewer about before you two get down to nuts and bolts, you'll have an opportunity to show interest in him or her later in the interview. That's when you'll be able to ask questions that show you are genuinely interested in your interviewer's thoughts about the organization, its culture, and what it takes to succeed in that environment.

So the good news is that, although the first impression that you make is important, it isn't your last chance to look good.

You'll have opportunities, throughout the interview, to show likability, to connect with your interviewer, and to have a conversation that both of you can enjoy.

TRY THIS

Think about how you act, and how other people react to you, when they meet you for the first time.

> Do you tend to **smile** at them, and if so, do they smile back?

> Are you the first person to **say hello**, and if so, do people respond in kind?

> Do you ever make **personal comments** to strangers? If so, are these met with appreciation or suspicion?

If you've never had a chance to experiment with talking to strangers, try it in your daily life. Factors like age, gender, race, and class will influence how well these interactions go; but your own attitude and expectations can also play a big role.

For example, as an older, middle-class white woman, I can start a conversation with anyone I want (because no one is afraid of me). This is a privilege I try to use wisely, by showing respect and open interest toward others; and if they're not being obnoxious, by responding with appreciation when someone starts a conversation with me.

Going around starting conversations can be trickier for people in other groups, notably young women and black men, but if you're able to talk to strangers, do it! These random interactions will hone your sense of what people find likable about you, and it's reassuring to know that you can make someone smile, or exchange a few sentences with pretty much anyone that you meet.

That's a skill worth developing — and not just because it will serve you well in job interviews!

TO SUM IT ALL UP...

> Get yourself, your clothes, and anything you plan to bring to your interview together the night before so that you're not harried about these details on the day of your interview.

> Choose clothes and accessories that are comfortable for you and match the organization's culture.

> When you first meet your interviewer, gather basic impressions about who they are and how they present themselves through their dress, attitude, and workspace.

> Make a positive first impression not just through your professional appearance and demeanor, but by smiling, offering a firm handshake, and if appropriate, commenting on some personal connection you've discovered.

Chapter 13:

To Connect with Your Interviewer, Make Conversation

You've probably been making conversation since you were a kid ("How was school today?" "OK. Can I have a snack?"), and you probably don't need me to explain how to do it.

But a funny thing happens to many people when they enter a job interview:

> They forget that *they* have power in this situation (re-read Chapter 1 if you need help remembering why this is true);

> They forget *they* have a personality, and focus instead on trying to be as bland and unobjectionable as they can; and

> They forget that, during an interview, they're *speaking to another human being!*

One benefit of **making conversation** with that other human being during your interview is that, in the process, you'll remember all those things!

You'll also get your mind off yourself and your anxieties for a few minutes. That's because, to successfully converse with a stranger requires that you **concentrate on them and what they're saying.** This is true whether you're making small talk or having a weightier exchange; and in either case, doing it is good for you.

It's also good for your interviewer. When you take some of the responsibility for making conversation off his or her shoulders, you're doing your interviewer a favor. Not every interviewer will notice or appreciate your efforts, but many of them will.

So How Do You Make Conversation?

Conversation is like volleyball, ping pong, tennis, or handball — in reverse!

If you've ever played one of those sports, you know that the object of the game is to hit a ball to your opponent in a way that makes it **difficult** for them to hit it back to you.

When you're making conversation, just turn that goal around:

Now you're trying to hit the (conversational) ball in a way that makes it **easy** for your conversational partner to "hit" it back to you.

If you and your interviewer are both playing that game, you'll find it easy to keep the conversational ball in motion. You'll both become more relaxed, and you'll probably learn something about each other.

In addition, when you make conversation with your interviewer, you're showing yourself to be confident, aware of your surroundings, and able to react appropriately to what's going on around you.

Start Your Interview with Small Talk

One of the best places to make conversation with your interviewer is right at the beginning, before you've gotten down to "official" business.

Because you don't know each other yet, this conversation will initially take the form of **small talk.**

Small talk is just what it sounds like: a discussion of inconsequential things like the weather, traffic, or to get more personal, the family picture on your interviewer's desk.

A lot of smart and thoughtful people shy away from small talk because it's... well, small. And it's true that, if you like your conversations to be meaningful, small talk — and particularly that early phase when you're grasping for something to talk about — can be painful.

But rather than resisting making small talk, I'm going to strongly suggest that you bite the bullet and **go with it.**

Why? Because small talk prepares *both you and your interviewer* for the more consequential talk that will follow. Or to put that differently, **small talk is your opportunity to check out your interviewer's conversational style before it really matters.**

So if your interviewer tosses you a small talk comment, *return it in a way that will keep the exchange going!*

Here's an example of what **not** to do:

Interviewer: Did you have any trouble getting here?
You: No.

Ouch!

Imagine your interviewer's inner wince. Since there's no way for him or her to pick up the conversational ball you just dropped, you are, in effect, forcing them to come up with something else to try to talk about.

I've suggested that you try to make your interviewer's job *easier* — and dropping a conversational ball that they've tossed to you doesn't qualify! Instead, to avoid irritating your interviewer, return the ball.

The Small Talk Formula: React and Return

Here are some things you could say in response to the small talk question, **"Did you have any trouble getting here?"**

> "No, it was easy. But I noticed there's a lot of new construction around here."

> "Traffic was worse than I expected, but fortunately I'd left enough time. Is it always that crowded on the 57?"

> "No, I just put on some music and enjoyed the scenery. This is a very pretty area."

> "It was fine, except for an accident near Johnson Bridge. Lots of rubbernecking."

See how easy that is? You **react** to what's been said, and then **return** the ball by asking another question or making a comment that invites *the interviewer* to respond.

And since there's always more than one way to respond to any comment, you don't have to worry about "getting it right." Just say something that's natural for you, and you'll be fine.

Here's an example of what that kind of extended exchange sounds like:

Example 1:

Interviewer: Did you have any trouble getting here?

You: No, it was easy; the directions were great. How's your commute? [*This is a variation on the world's best small-talk response, "How about you?"*]

Interviewer: Not bad. I take the train, so at least I get some reading done.

You: Really. What do you like to read?

Interviewer: Mostly bestsellers. I just finished the new J.D. Robb; have you heard of her?

You: I read everything she writes. I think the new one is one of her best.

Interviewer: As good as *Origin in Death*?

You: Well, nothing is that good, but it's pretty close!

Now before you go yelling "Foul!" (because, really, how often will an interviewer share one of your favorite hobbies!), just be aware that *small talk will work even if you don't have the same taste in reading, or anything else.* **As in the interview itself, the point is not for you to know everything.** The point is for you to connect with your interviewer by making conversation, as in this example:

> **Example 2:**

Interviewer: Did you have any trouble getting here?

You: No, it was easy; the directions were great. How's *your* commute?

Interviewer: Not bad. I take the train, so at least I get some reading done.

You: Really. What do you like to read?

Interviewer: Mostly bestsellers. I just finished the new J.D. Robb; have you heard of her?

You: I've seen that name, but I haven't read anything by her. Are they mysteries?

Interviewer: They're sort of futuristic cop procedurals with some romance.

You: That sounds like fun.

Interviewer: It is. She's a great storyteller.

Even if you hate bestselling fiction, you can still **use small talk to connect**, as in this last example:

Example 3:

Interviewer: Did you have any trouble getting here?

You: No, it was easy; the directions were great. How's *your* commute?

Interviewer: Not bad. I take the train, so at least I get some reading done.

You: Really. What do you like to read?

Interviewer: Mostly bestsellers. I just finished the new J.D. Robb; have you heard of her?

You: No, I haven't. What does she write?

Interviewer: They're futuristic cop procedurals with some romance.

You: (smile) I don't think I've ever read anything like that. I usually go for non-fiction.

Interviewer: Yeah? What kind of stuff?

You: Science, technology. Right now I'm reading a book about how to create medicine that works with your individual DNA.

Interviewer: That sounds more futuristic than J.D. Robb.

You: Yeah, it *is* kind of like science fiction. Everyone agrees that this is the future of medicine, but nobody really knows how it's going to work.

You can see from these examples that, whether or not you and your interviewer share the same taste in reading (or anything else!), *expressing an interest in each other's taste* will help you settle down to business feeling much more at ease about talking to each other.

That's a big payoff for two minutes of small talk!

And the beauty of the **react and return approach to small talk** is that, even if one of you doesn't like to read *anything*, you can still shift the conversation to the more general topic of hobbies, or how you pass the time during your commute, or whatever comes to mind.

The endgame is not to discover mutual interests (though you might). It's to **keep the conversational ball going** so that both of you can get a sense of the other person's conversational style.

"You're Never Fully Dressed Without a Smile"

In the Broadway show **Annie,** Li'l Orphan Annie and her friends sing a song — written by Charles Strouse and Martin Charnin © 1977 — with these lyrics:

> "Who cares what they're wearing
> On Main Street or Saville Row?
> It's what you wear from ear to ear
> And not from head to toe
> That matters"

Saville Row was (maybe still is) where hyper-rich Londoners went to shop, and the point is that — whether you're rich, poor, or in between — you're not presenting yourself to full advantage if you're not smiling.

To that, I would add that you'll always seem more involved in a conversation if you're making eye contact with the other person. And **nowhere are a smile and good eye contact more important than in a job interview.** Together, they are the perfect way to let the other person know that you're enjoying their conversation.

Which raises the interesting question: What if you're *not* enjoying your interviewer's conversation, of feeling any connection at all?

Not Every Conversation Will Click

In spite of your sincere smile, your open mind, and your best efforts at making small talk, you and your interviewer may just not hit it off.

If this happens, **it's not your fault.**

It takes two people to create a conversation, and — in addition to the possibility that you and your interviewer are just a terrible match-up — it's also possible that your interviewer isn't interested in connecting with you, or doesn't have the social skills to do so.

Certainly give it more than one try. But if you're tried several times to get a conversation going... if you've smiled more than once and your smile isn't being returned... if your efforts to find topics of interest to discuss are being ignored or rebuffed by the interviewer... you've done everything that you can do.

In that case disengage, take a mental step back, and rely on courtesy, professionalism, and preparation to get you through the rest of this interview.

Whatever you do, though, **don't burn any bridges** by being rude, sarcastic, or fatalistic. People act strangely for all kinds of reasons, and even if the interview seemed like a total loss to you, you don't know how things are going to turn out.

As we discussed in Chapter 4, if your interviewer seems to adore you, that's no guarantee that you'll get the job; and if your interviewer has all the warmth of an igloo, that doesn't mean that you won't.

As famed New York Yankee catcher Yogi Berra once said, "It ain't over till it's over."

The Role of Conversation During the Middle of Your Interview

I've suggested that your interview start with some small talk, initiated either by you or by your interviewer. This can help to warm both of you up, and set the stage for a more relaxed and cordial Q&A.

But once you've entered that Q&A, your goal is no longer to **make conversation**, it's to answer the questions your interviewer asks in a way that **demonstrates you're the person they should hire**, by satisfying the interviewer's concerns while putting yourself in the best possible light.

If your interviewer wants to focus on a point you've made and turn it into a conversation, go along with that.

But unless he or she hits the conversational ball back to you, just finish your answer... stop talking... and wait to see what they ask next.

At the End, Make Conversation About the Organization or Job

Just as the beginning of an interview is a good time for you to take the conversational lead, so is the end. But the conversation you make at the end of an interview will be more substantive than the small talk you made earlier.

In fact, your main goal here is to **ask questions that show your interest in the organization.** This is where the list of **Your Questions for the Interviewer** from Chapter 6 comes into play.

If some of your questions lead to conversational exchanges, that's great; but don't force things. As always, take your interviewer's lead and stay flexible and centered, confident in your knowledge that *you're* **the person they should hire.**

Here are some examples of how this might play out following a question that you ask:

Example 1:

You: If I'm lucky enough to get this job, how many people will I be supervising?

Interviewer: I don't know.

Again, ouch!

Your conversational partner just let the ball drop, and that's no fun. Earlier in this chapter, I suggested that you should *not* do this to your poor interviewer, and now you can see why.

If the interviewer does this to you, stay cool, calm and collected and go on to your next question.

Example 2:

In this example, you're able to get information and have a cordial exchange with the interviewer:

You: If I'm lucky enough to get this job, how many people will I be supervising?

Interviewer: That team has traditionally been six people — three copywriters and three graphic artists — but because of the reorganization, it's hard to know if that's going to change.

You: But you think it's likely to be something like six people?

Interviewer: That would be my best guess right now.

Example 3:

Finally, here's an example that goes beyond exchanging information. You probably wouldn't push like this unless you already felt a rapport with your interviewer. But if you *do* feel that rapport, it makes sense to try for a real interaction, using the React and Respond skills that you just learned.

You: If I'm lucky enough to get this job, how many people will I be supervising?

Interviewer: I don't know exactly. That team has traditionally been six people — three copywriters and three graphic artists — but because of the reorganization, it's hard to know if that's going to change.

You: Well, if it stays at around six people, that'll be great. I think that's the optimal number of people for a team.

Interviewer: Why do you say that?

You: With six people, you can supervise everyone closely, and the group is small enough for them to feel like a unit. But that's also a big enough group to create a lot of possible combinations of talent, so nobody gets stale.

Interviewer: That's an interesting way to look at it. It sounds like you would enjoy having a small team.

You: I would. Small teams can be very productive. Speaking of which **[here comes your next question]**, would my team have any creative autonomy? Or would it be working within strict guidelines?

See how that goes? By pushing things to a deeper level, you've given your interviewer more information about how you would do the job, and even invited him or her to *imagine* you in the role of team leader ("...would my team...?")

Yes, this kind of comment can be a risk. But the benefits are potentially tremendous.

Putting Yourself Into the Role

Here's another example of how you can invite your interviewer to picture you in the job they need to fill. In this case, notice that the conversation:

> Begins with a question that suggests you might get the job, and

> Ends with a comment that assumes you almost have it!

You: One thing I wanted to ask is, what do you think it's going to take for me, or whoever gets this job, to succeed in the ER Nurse position?

Interviewer: I would say that flexibility is number one.

You: Do you mean in terms of the schedule?

Interviewer: Well the schedule is important, as you know. Your shifts will change and you may have to come in early, stay late, whatever. But I really meant being able to jump from one thing that you're doing to the next, because you're never able to really do just one thing.

You: That's not a problem. Every ER is like that. What about working with the physicians?

Interviewer: That's another area where flexibility counts. We've got some very buttoned-down physicians who'll make sure you understand exactly what they want. And then there are others you'll be chasing down the hall trying to get them to explain their instructions to you.

You: It sounds like I'd better wear roller skates to work.

Interviewer: That's actually not a bad idea!

Putting It All Together

I wish that I could give you a one-size-fits-all script that you could follow to make conversation and connect with the interviewer at *each* of your job interviews.

But one size **doesn't** fit all when conversation is involved — which is why you need to stay alert and really *listen* to what your interviewer is saying. This is true not just when you first walk into the room, but throughout your entire interview.

Here are some tips to help you stay present:

> **Stay focused on your interviewer's face** when you're speaking, and listen attentively whenever he or she speaks.

> **Jot down important things that your interviewer says,** along with questions you may want to ask later in the interview.

> **Have your own questions, some notes that will help you answer questions, and your resume in front of you.** This isn't a memorization contest. Don't add to the stress you're already feeling by requiring yourself to remember every fact in your resume, or exactly what questions you planned to ask. Check off the questions as you ask them.

> **Be in the moment, to the greatest extent you can be.** What this means is that if something happens that you don't like — you forget part of an answer, or stumble over a word — try to recover as quickly as possible by *focusing on the thing that happens next.* If you overreact to a perceived "mistake," you're in danger of missing the interviewer's next question, which is a new opportunity to be your best.

And most of all,

DON'T FORGET that **your goal is *not* to be perfect.** Your GOAL is to **demonstrate that you're the person they should hire.**

TRY THIS

Many people hate the term "role play," but it's the phrase that accurately describes how to practice for an interview. (Or we could just call it "practicing"!) Here's how to do it:

> First, **choose a partner you can practice with.** This person can be a friend, a colleague, a family member, or another

(continues on next page)

job seeker like yourself. I'm a fan of practicing with smart middle school (junior high school) students. Unlike adults, they won't push you to make your answers more complex or inclusive, and they'll tell you if they don't understand what you're saying.

> When you've chosen a practice partner, sit down in a place with no distractions, and **act out the interview as if you were putting on a play.**

> Start by having your partner play the interviewer. He or she should have a **list of possible questions to ask you**, and can also make up questions on the fly. Be sure to include questions that you *haven't* practiced answering on the list!

> Act out the interview several times, with your practice partner taking on **different interviewer personalities** — one that's sympathetic, one that's impatient and critical, etc. And don't worry about the quality of anyone's acting; this is a *practice session*, not an audition for a Broadway show!

> To wrap things up, **switch roles** and play the interviewer for a few minutes. The more you understand your interviewer's challenges, the more smoothly your interview will go.

TO SUM IT ALL UP...

> Conversation, which is like **a game of ping-pong in reverse**, is a great way for you to connect with and learn more about your interviewer.

> **Practice using all of these skills in several rounds of "role play"** with another person, including one in which you play the interviewer.

> Early in the interview, **make small talk by reacting to what your interviewer says, and then returning the conversational ball to them.**

> In the long middle of your interview, don't try to make conversation. Instead, **stay focused on your interviewer's questions, and answer them the best you can** using everything you've learned from this book.

> At the end of your interview, use the questions that you've prepared to **show your interest in the organization**, and learn more about it — and deepen the conversation if that seems appropriate.

> Throughout the interview, **maintain a flexible attitude**, smile at your interviewer and make eye contact. And even if things don't click between you, don't panic or give up hope, because "it ain't over till it's over."

Chapter 14:

How to Ace Phone and Skype Interviews Without Tripping Over the Technology

There may be an occasional exception to this, but in general, phone interviews are hoops that you have to jump through on your way to the **in-person interview.**

Why do "they" put you through this?

Well, suppose that 10 well-qualified candidates have applied for a position, but the organization thinks it's too expensive or time-consuming to meet with more than, say, three of them. How do they choose which seven to eliminate?

Phone Interviews.

What this means is that *a 10-minute (or so) phone call will determine whether or not you have a shot at this job.*

Never Take a Phone Interview Lightly

Because of that, don't make the mistake of underestimating how important your phone interview can be. **Prepare** and **practice** for this interview as thoroughly as you would for any other — because there won't *be* any other interview unless you pass this first test.

To ace your phone interview:

❯ Spend time sprucing up your **Avatar** (your best self).

❯ Carefully **research** the organization and, if possible, the person who'll be interviewing you.

❯ Make lists of **generic, awkward and job-related questions**, and decide on **some questions you'll ask** about the organization or job.

❯ Work out answers that **demonstrate you're the person they should hire.**

❯ **Practice the interview with a trusted partner** — and do it on the phone, not in person.

That last point is important: *Practice for your phone interview on the phone.*

Do this so that you get a real-time feeling for what it will take to do the interview well. And do it **because phone interviews present technical difficulties that in-person interviews don't.**

You want to identify and solve those problems *before* the actual interview.

The Special Challenges of Phone Interviews

To sound great on the phone, you'll have to overcome these challenges:

❯ **You're not in the room with your interviewer.** You can't read his facial expressions, and he can't see your sincere smile. Eye contact, one of the main ways that people connect, is eliminated.

❯ **The sound quality on phones can be lousy.** This is particularly true with cell phones (which we'll get to in a minute), but it can also be an issue if your landline has call waiting or if you're speaking in a place where there's background noise. Bad sound isn't an *aesthetic* concern; it means that *your interviewer will have trouble **hearing** you* (or vice versa), which makes for an awkward exchange.

> **Conversely, phone conversations amplify undesirable sounds.** If you're chewing gum, smoking, drinking coffee, typing on a keyboard, sniffling, walking around, making side comments to other people in the room, even shuffling papers or breathing directly into the receiver, it's likely your interviewer will pick up these sounds.

> **You have to be more cautious about what you say.** Just as nuance can get lost in emails or text messages (is she teasing me, or being snide?), it can get lost on the phone. So you need to play it safer than you would in a face-to-face interaction. Slang, irony, idiosyncratic language, statements with multiple layers of meaning, and even PG-13 humor can fall flat or actually backfire.

> **Phone interviews are short.** You have less time to make a good impression, and if you say something that doesn't put you in the best possible light, you have less time to recover your composure and make a more positive impression.

Remember that — unlike in a face-to-face interview, where you're already a contender for the job — the point of a phone interview is **to eliminate you from the list of possible hires.**

Don't give your phone interviewer the excuse they need to cross you off that list!

Act As If You're Talking Face-to-Face

If you use only one tip from this chapter, here it is: **When you're on a phone interview, act is if you're talking face-to-face.**

These actions will put you into a face-to-face mindset:

> **Get dressed for the interview.** Wear what you would be wearing if you were going to the organization's offices, and groom yourself accordingly.

> Use the strategies from Chapter 12 that you would use to **prepare for an in-person interview.** These include getting a good night's sleep the night before, eating a good meal the day of, and warming up your voice (and your Avatar) before you get on the phone call.

> **Stand up for the interview.** Even though you wouldn't stand for a face-to-face interview, do it now. Your energy will be better, and your attention will stay more focused if you're standing tall rather than sitting at your desk.

> **Smile a lot.** If you're thinking, "They can't see me smile!" remember that there are other senses — and *hearing* is one of our most acute. Whether or not people realize it consciously, they will respond to the *sound* of your smile. (Smiling changes the way you sound, just as opening your mouth or articulating more carefully does.)

> **Invoke the interviewer.** If you're a literal person or an extravert, print the interviewer's picture (or any photo of what you think the interviewer may look like), paste it at eye level while you're standing, and *talk to the picture* during your interview. If you're an introvert (meaning that you're more energized by your inner world than by outside stimuli), you can get the same effect by *imagining* your interviewer; and since you're alone, it's okay to shut your eyes to help you concentrate. But either way, stay focused on your interviewer's real or imagined face, as you would if they were present.

If You're Using a Cell Phone, Use It With Care

Because landline reception is almost always better than cell phone sound, it's best to do a phone interview in a quiet place with **a landline**, it that's possible.

When you can't arrange to call from a landline:

> **Pick your location for this call in advance.** The spot should be quiet, private, and have the best possible reception. **Do not** take an interview call in public, and particularly not in a coffee shop or while driving your car.

> During the call, **speak directly into your cell phone mike.** Don't let your phone (and therefore your voice) wander.

> Do your best to **not rush, mumble, or let your voice drop off** at the end of comments.

> **Slow down** and leave a pause after each comment or idea. This makes it easier for the other person to hear you, and is a best practice for **any** conversation, but particularly for cell phone calls!

Whether You're On a Cell or a Landline, Use Good Telephone Manners

Whatever the quality of your phone connection, make the interview call go better by observing these common sense courtesies:

> **If *you're* placing the call, identify yourself when they pick up.** Say, "Hi, this is [your name]. I'm calling to speak with [interviewer's name]." or "Hello, I'm [your name]. Is this [interviewer's name]?"

> **If *they're* placing the call, greet them warmly.** "Hi, John [or Mr. Johnson]. This is [your full name]. It's great to hear from

you," or "I've been looking forward to our conversation." If he or she asks, "Are you ready for this interview?" say yes, and don't equivocate!

> **Be prepared for a moment of small talk.** Follow your interviewer's lead on this, but don't be surprised if — even in a short interview — they want to get a feel for your personality before plunging into their list of questions. (Go back to Chapter 13 to refresh your memory of how to make small talk.)

> **If you're uncertain about anything, ask.** Since you're missing important visual cues, it's reasonable that you might mis-hear or misunderstand a question. If you think that's happened, say, "I'm sorry, would you repeat that, please?" And if you're not sure you've answered to their satisfaction — maybe because they aren't reacting — it's fine to ask for direction, with a question like, "Would you like me to go into more detail about how we solved that problem?"

> **Handle interruptions graciously.** Unless your house is burning down, don't let anything on your end interrupt this call. But if your interviewer asks you to hold for a minute, graciously agree. He or she may be distracted when they come back on the line, so be prepared to remind them of where you were in the conversation.

Skype Interviews: Taking Remote to the Next Level

In some ways, being interviewed on Skype or any other videoconferencing system combines the worst of both worlds.

You're subject to the uncertainties that technology brings — bad connections, missed information, poor quality sound or visuals, the lack of immediacy that comes when you're not in the room together — and you're also *being observed* as you cope with not just the technology but the interview itself.

Still, with the right preparation, you can make a Skype interview work for you; and a good Skype interview will set you far apart from other candidates who haven't mastered the medium.

Just As You Would with a Phone Interview, Solve the Tech Problems that Come with Skype First

> **Get the best possible Internet connection.** As with phone interviews, the best location for conducting this call is in your home — provided that your home has a place that's private and reliably connected to the Internet. Run advance tests to find that spot, or borrow a friend's place. Internet cafés and public libraries are not the right venues for a job interview.

> **Minimize the clutter that your interviewer will see in the background during your call.** A Skype camera doesn't just capture *you*, it captures whatever's behind you in the room. So make sure your interviewer isn't looking at last night's dishes, an unmade bed, or even a disorganized stack of work materials. That isn't the image you want to project. And be sure that your Skype icon (the image people see when you're not on camera) is ***professional***. Daffy Duck just isn't going to cut it!

> **Backlighting is best**, which means that the light in your location should be *behind you*. If your interview location is bright and sunny, count your blessings. But if, like most of us, you have to use artificial lighting to be clearly visible, avoid lights that shine down from directly above you (they'll make you look shadowy, even shifty) or that send off a bright glare from right beside you. The best lighting is strong enough to illuminate, but far enough away to give a diffuse, general effect. Test this in advance of your interview at the time of day when your call is scheduled.

> **Put your camera at eye level.** When you speak with someone face-to-face, you're generally not looking way up or **way** down at them, so place your camera at eye level to give a face-to-face impression, even if this means raising

your laptop on a pile of books. Remember, too, that **not every Skype call is a video call!** Check with your interviewer before turning your camera on so that you're not stuck looking at their icon while they watch your every on-camera move.

> If you are both on camera, however, **move the picture of your interviewer's face so that it's right below your own camera.** Again, this will help create the impression that you and your interviewer are literally face-to-face.

> And if for some reason you are **not** able to move your interviewer's image to just below the camera on the computer, **ignore the person and talk to the camera.** The reason for this is that **your interviewer will see what the camera "sees."** If you're talking straight at the camera, you will *appear* to be looking the interviewer right in the eye. If you're talking to an image of your interviewer that's in a lower portion of your screen, you will *appear* to be speaking with your eyes cast down and away from them.

Stay Calm If There Are Technical Glitches

Sometimes, in spite of everyone's best efforts, videoconferencing software will let you down. This, like everything else in your interview, is a chance to demonstrate that you're calm, confident, and able to roll with the punches. *After all, setbacks are part of any job, and this is your interviewer's chance to observe how you deal with them.*

So be as relaxed and helpful as possible, make suggestions if you have any, but let your interviewer solve the problem. If they offer to place the video call again, agree. If they suggest switching to another videoconferencing system or a phone call, agree. If they decide to reschedule the interview, agree.

Don't show nervousness, frustration, or negative emotion. And don't react (except with mild sympathy) if your interviewer shows them.

When Your Skype Interview Is the "Big One"

While it's rare for a phone interview to be final, a Skype interview may actually be substituting for an in-person interview that can't occur because of time, distance, or cost.

When this is the case (or you even suspect that it might be), arm yourself with all the information, cheat sheets, and aids — water, a mint, whatever you think will be useful — that you would bring to a full-length in-person interview.

Settle down, relax, and try to pace yourself. And just as with a face-to-face interview, *stay focused on what's happening right now* instead of brooding over an imagined "mistake," or worrying about what question will be next.

"I'm Very Interested. What Happens Next?"

If you're not clear about what will happen after this interview, wait until the end, then ask. Just make your question general, so that you're not putting your interviewer on the spot. "What happens next?" is a better question than "Are you going to call me?"

You may also want to take this opportunity to tell your interviewer that you're excited about the job, look forward to hearing from them soon, or would love to work for their organization. Don't force those sentiments, but if you're truly feeling enthusiastic, feel free to say so with a confident smile.

While you might think these points are obvious, remember that *a lot can get lost in translation over phone or Skype.* It never hurts to state your interest in a casual but sincere way.

TRY THIS

While it's critically important to practice for any interview, *it's even more important when technology is involved.* Treat these run-throughs as "tech rehearsals," and be sure that you're comfortable with your system and set-up before the date of your interview.

You can even practice how you'll react if something goes wrong during your phone or Skype interview. Remember that, while you can't always control your dog, your kids, the ambulance siren outside your window, or even a faulty Internet connection, **you *can* control how you react to these disruptions.**

Try for calm and confident! And even if nothing goes wrong during your interview, you'll feel better knowing that you've practiced and prepared for the possibility.

TO SUM IT ALL UP...

> Phone and Skype interviews add both **technical and social challenges**, so be sure to prepare for them in advance.

> In addition to how you would otherwise prepare, **practice using your technology and compensating for its limits.**

> **Imagine that you're talking with your interviewer face-to-face.** The more present and natural you can be, the better this interview will go.

> Even though phone and Skype interviews are often preliminary tests that you must pass to get the "real" interview, **treat them with the same seriousness** you would a face-to-face interview.

Chapter 15:
You Did It!
Now Follow Up With a Great Thank You Note

Congratulations!!

You made it through the job interview, and now you're ready to hit the nearest gym, or couch, or club to unwind.

But not so fast. You've got one more thing to do before your job interview is totally finished: ***You need to write a thank you note!*** This is probably not the thing you most want to do right now, but it's a *necessary last step* in your interview process.

That's because a great thank you note accomplishes three important things. It:

> Prompts your interviewer to **remember you in a positive way**;
> Reminds him or her that **you're the person they should hire**; and
> Gives you a chance to **affirm your interest in the job**.

More on each of those benefits in a minute. But first...

What *Is* a Thank You Note?

Thank you notes are brief, handwritten cards that you write with a pen, put a stamp on, and deliver through the postal service.

Does that sound retro? It should — because thank you notes are meant to evoke the unhurried appreciation that people gave each other (at least theoretically) in pre-Internet days. Apart from what your note says, the very act of sending a thank you note shows that you are so grateful to this other person that you're willing to almost step out of time to thank them.

You just don't get that effect by tweeting!

So what are the qualities of a great thank you note?

A Great Thank You Note Makes Your Interviewer Feel Good About Himself or Herself — and You!

Assuming that your note is crafted well (and I'll show you how to do that in this chapter), it should make your interviewer feel good.

That's because you're going to tell them that *they did a good job interviewing you.* We all want to be praised, or at least acknowledged for doing our jobs well; and we generally feel good when someone notices. We also feel good about *the person* who notices, and we're inclined to think that they must be particularly smart or perceptive!

At the very least, when someone takes the trouble to thank us in a warm and appropriate way, we'll probably find them pretty darned likable.

And remember, ***people like to hire people they like.***

A Great Thank You Note Lets You Re-State Your Interest, and Reminds Them that *You're the Best Person for the Job*

You may wonder why re-stating your interest is necessary. After all, you *applied* for the job. You *interviewed* for the job. Obviously you **want** the job.

But this fact, that looms so large for you, may not be clear to your interviewer.

> Maybe she's distracted by a fight with her spouse, or some depressing reversal in her own life. Maybe she has a cold.

> Maybe he was impressed by you but didn't sense the kind of personal commitment or excitement he likes to see from a job candidate.

> Or maybe, after interviewing several people, he or she is just fuzzy on the details of how your particular interview went.

In these cases (and many others you can probably think of), restating your strong interest in the job will help you *stand out* from other applicants. And there is *no case* in which a professional, matter-of-fact statement of interest can hurt you.

A great think you note also reminds your interviewer that *you're* the person they should hire.

Importantly, *you* don't remind the interviewer of this; *your thank you note* does the job for you by refreshing his or her memory of your interview.

Of course, this is a fine line to walk. But fortunately it's not hard, once you know how.

Before we go to that step-by-step process, here are two commonly asked questions about thank you notes:

> ### Can I just email my note?

It's fine to email your thank you note if you want to look like everyone else they've interviewed!

But if you want to make a stronger impression, go the extra mile by writing your note on paper, and mailing it with a stamp.

> ### Should I write my note in advance?

No. Job hunters are sometimes advised to bring a pre-written thank you note to their interview, and drop it off as they're leaving. The problem with this approach is that, since you haven't met the interviewer yet, a pre-written note would be vague and general.

I suggest that you write your note *just after* the interview, when you have something unique and specific to say.

Here's how to prepare — before, during, and after the interview — to write a killer thank you note:

Before Your Interview, Collect the Materials You'll Need for a Thank You Note

Before your interview (whether it's a week, a month, or an hour before):

> Buy an attractive **note card** from a card shop or a high-end drug store. The front should not be "humorous," though attractive or interesting photos or drawings are OK. And there shouldn't be anything written inside, because that part is going to come from you.

> Buy a **stamp**, or a "book" of 20. Stamps are sold at the post office, at USPS.com, and in drug stores and large retail stores. They might even be available in your grocery store.

> Buy a **pen** that feels good in your hand. It's easier to write a note if you like the tool you're writing it with. And don't worry if you haven't written anything by hand in decades; it will come back to you.

During the Interview, Get the Information You'll Need for Your Thank You Note

Again, the goal is to make this process easy. So during your interview, remember to:

> Get a **business card** from every person who was present, whether they asked you questions or not.

> If their cards don't include the company's **mailing address**, ask the receptionist for it on your way out — it may not be the street address you came to — and get the correct floor number and zip code.

After the Interview, Organize Your Thoughts Before You Write

Before you sit down to write your thank you note, you may want to collect your thoughts and do a general "debrief" on the interview.

How you do this debrief will depend, in part, on whether you're an Extravert who gets energy from the outer world of people, places, and things, or an Introvert who gets energy from quiet reflection:

> If you're an **Introvert**, you'll probably find a quiet corner in the building lobby, a nearby coffee shop, or just sit in your car so that you can mull over what happened and write down a few thoughts.

> If you're an **Extravert**, you'll probably want to call a friend and tell them everything that everyone said.

In either case, look for specific things that struck you, such as:

> A **piece of information or word of encouragement** that your interviewer offered

> A **question** that he or she answered particularly well;

> A **quality** that the interviewer had — for example, patience, or enthusiasm, or calmness — that impressed you or put you at ease.

What Do You Think Your Interviewer Enjoyed?

In my book on public speaking, ***SPEAK LIKE YOURSELF... No, Really! Follow Your Strengths and Skills to Great Public Speaking***, I argue that every "speech" begins with an "audience analysis."

In this case, your "audience" is the person, or people, who interviewed you. To put them solidly in mind, ask yourself:

> Did they seem to enjoy our conversation (how did they show it)?

> Where, in particular, did we connect (around a hobby, a work challenge, a topic of conversation)?

> Was their interviewing style more on the "warm and friendly" or more on the "strictly business" end of the scale? (This will help you write your note in a style that your interviewer will find comfortable.)

Now Use "The Rule of 3" to Draft Your Note

Three sentences, plus a date, a greeting, and a close, are all you need to get this thank you note done.

But before you commit to writing your card, take a piece of notebook or scratch paper and write what's called a "first draft" (meaning you can change it before the final version).

Then, on the left, write, "Dear [Their Name]." If the person was super friendly, a first name will do ("Dear Mary"); if they were super formal, use their title ("Dear Vice President Jones"). If they were middle-of-the-road (not particularly formal or friendly), your best bet is to use "Mr." or "Ms." and their last name ("Dear Mr. Jones," or "Dear Ms. [or Mrs.] Jones").

Then write your note by following this structure:

Sentence #1:
Thank the person for meeting with you.

> If you liked them, or if they were particularly friendly, you can say something like "Thank you for making my interview today so pleasant."

> If they were more businesslike, just say something like, "Thank you for taking the time to meet with me today."

Sentence #2:
Mention something that you liked about the interview.

> If they were personal or friendly, say something personal, such as, "I particularly enjoyed our talk about [whatever you particularly enjoyed talking about]."

> If they were more businesslike, say something businesslike, such as, "I was glad to learn more about [name of the organization]."

Sentence #3:
Repeat your interest in the job — but don't repeat your qualifications or act as if the interview is still going on!

> Friendly version: "I would be thrilled to work for [name of organization], and hope to meet you again as a colleague."

> Business version: "I am now even more interested in working with [name of organization], and appreciate your help with the process."

Here's what those two notes look like when you put it all together:

Friendlier Version:

> Thank you for making my interview today so pleasant. I particularly enjoyed our talk about [team-building, budget planning, automobile maintenance, etc]. I would be thrilled to work for [name of organization], and hope to meet you again as a colleague.

More Businesslike Version:

> Thank you for taking the time to meet with me today. I was glad to learn more about [name of organization]. I am now even more interested in working with [name of organization], and appreciate your help with the process.

Proofread Your Note Before Copying and Sending It

Just as you wouldn't send a resume with spelling mistakes or errors of grammar, make sure that your thank you note is clean and correct. (And if you're not a good proofreader, ask someone who is to look it over.)

Once you've done that, **copy your words onto the card you brought along**, put the card in its envelope, write your interviewer's address (include the title from their business card), put the stamp on the envelope (with the address facing you, the stamp goes in the upper right-hand corner), find the nearest mail box — they're often on street corners, ask someone if you don't see one — and toss your note into the mailbox.

A day or two from now, your interviewer is going to be pleasantly reminded of you.

Don't Lose the Lesson, or the Celebration

I know I said that you could hit the gym (or the couch or the club) once your thank you note was mailed — and you can.

But on your way from the mailbox to your next destination, give yourself another minute to think about how things went today:

> What **went better** than you expected?

> Where were you **particularly effective**?

> Is there something in particular that you'd like to **improve**?

> **What steps** do you need to take to make your next interview go even better?

Grab those thoughts, insights, and suggestions — and then put them aside for later.

Right now, you deserve to kick back and celebrate your own success.

Congratulations on your hard work and great attitude. You're on the right road, so keep moving forward and **you *will* get the job in 2014!**

TRY THIS

For many people, the period following a job interview — when you're waiting to hear back from the organization — can be agonizing.

Even if you feel like you're in limbo and are checking your cell phone fifty times a day to see if your interviewer has contacted you, keep yourself and your job search on track during this period.

Make a checklist of things that need doing (lunch with a contact? more LinkedIn research? a new version of your resume?) and do at least one of them every day. You owe that to yourself and your job search, because the more actions you take, the more likely it is that one of them will succeed!

TO SUM IT ALL UP...

> Thank you notes are effective reminders of why **you're the best person for the job.** Send one following every interview.

> Take the thank you note supplies you need to each interview, but don't actually write your card until afterwards.

> Sit and think (if you're an Introvert) or talk to a friend (if you're an Extravert) about specific things that went well during your interview.

> Then write a draft note, based on the three-sentence templates in this chapter.

> Proofread your note, copy it onto the notecard, and mail it.

> Finally, **think about the lessons you've learned, and the steps you'll take next.** Don't let your job search grind to a halt while you wait to hear about your last interview. Instead, set your sights on the next interview, and keep moving forward toward your goal.

BONUS CHAPTER:
HR, Recruiting, and Career Experts Share the One Thing They Wish You Knew

I'm deeply grateful to each of the HR, Recruiting, and Career Coaching Professionals who shared their insights to enrich this book. Their tips are tactical, practical, and filled with wisdom. They will help you GET THE JOB in 2014!

"Ask them, 'Why is the job open?'"

> —Mark P. Sneff, SPHR, Global Vice President Human Resources, Premier Research International

"The best job search technique is about relationships — people hire people. Focus on listening, connecting, helping, and following up and you'll build a solid foundation for your career."

> —Caroline Ceniza-Levine, Career Expert, SixFigureStart®

"Don't go to an interview empty-handed. Compile a short list of questions, ones that demonstrate your knowledge and interest in the company and the job. When the interviewer asks if you have any questions, you won't be caught off guard."

> —Elizabeth Garone, BBC Capital Career Coach Columnist and *Wall Street Journal* Contributing Writer

"Be yourself, be honest, and open. Don't try to be who you think we want to see. 90% of the time an interviewer will see right through that and you will be unsuccessful; and the 10% of the time it works, you will be miserable if you get the role. If you have to come in everyday masking the real you and/or what you believe, you won't last long and will find yourself back in the interview seat very quickly."

—Kevin M. Horan, Vice President, Human Resources and Corporate Services, International Lease Finance Corporation

"It's not about YOU. Interviews are not your time to dish out every element of your background with the hopes that they hear something that is interesting. Pivot everything on their job description, their needs, their company and your fit for THEM. Prepare your answers to be relevant to THEM."

—Dana Manciagli, Global Career Expert, Speaker, Coach, Author of *Cut the Crap, Get a Job!*

"This advice relates to your 'emotional intelligence.' Know yourself well. Be comfortable and confident in that self-knowledge. Make that your most basic and fundamental comfort zone. In any kind of interview situation, always remain your most comfortable and confident self, relying on that self-knowledge and self-awareness. You will then be cool, poised and always be at your best."

—Rob Duval, Chief Human Resources Officer, Bradley Hospital (a Lifespan Partner)

"Hire your boss...first. The company, the money and opportunity may be phenomenal but if you don't seriously connect with the person who is going to control your destiny for the next several years, you'll end up regretting it. So pay attention to your spider sense and if you're unsure, 'break bread' with your future boss and see if there is a there there."

—Allison Hemming, Top Gun, The Hired Guns

"All interviews are about three questions: Can you do the job? Will you love the job? Do I want to work with you? Be ready to address those three often unspoken questions with your answers."

—Celia Currin, Partner, The Art of the Career

Be honest during the interview. Recruiters are generally highly experienced and skilled at interviewing and they are able to identify when a candidate is responding with "what should be" compared to what the truth is. Everyone has successes and failures, and to try and present only the positive detracts from the candidates credibility and serves as a warning sign to the interviewer."

—Larry R. Reese, Sr. Vice President, Human Resources,
Blood Systems, Inc.

"Past success is the best predictor of future success, and experienced employers and hiring managers know this to be true. Thus, it's important to review your experiences and skills gained in your past jobs, and think about how those skills would translate into the new job for which you are interviewing. At the end of the day, employers want to hire people who can think things through intelligently and independently, so help them to connect the dots on how your experience would translate to their specific issues and needs."

—Jennifer Bezoza, Leadership Coach,
Jennifer Bezoza Consulting

"Know as much as you can about your interviewer: Their generation, their basic LinkedIn profile, their personality type, what motivates them."

—Anne Loehr, Director, Anne Loehr & Associates

"Research the company you are interviewing with. I always began an interview with thanking them for coming in and then I ask, 'So where did you see our ad and what do you know about our company?'"

—Daniel Poray, Director of Human Resources,
Remington Hotels

"The screening starts before the interview. The way you conduct yourself the minute you walk into the company you are applying to matters."

—Raul Argudin, Director, Human Resources, Bloomingdale's

"If the interviewer is terrible and does not really interview you, you may want to 'interview yourself' by giving him or her a strong sense of who you are and what skills you bring. It is critical you leave them knowing who you are even if they do not ask, otherwise you may not be differentiated from the other candidates."

— Patrick J. Mulvey, Human Resources Consultant, PJM & Associates

"ATTITUDE is everything. By "attitude" I mean passion, positivity, honesty, work ethic, competitiveness and tenacity. I have learned after literally thousands of interviews that skills can be faked, but "attitude" is either there or it is not. Employers can teach skills; no one can teach someone to have a fire and conviction to succeed that they do not already possess. Most successful leaders and companies I know hire for attitude first and skills second. Keeping this in mind, job seekers need to take every interaction to convey to an Interviewer/Recruiter why they have the right attitude. Doing so makes up for so many other things."

—Jason Leonard, VP Human Resources, Caliber Home Loans

" Clearly, each of us has unique abilities and talents. However, some people are better storytellers than others. Once you've uncovered your strengths and skills, put them in context so that the interviewer can gain an accurate picture of who you really are and what you can contribute to the organization. Leave no gaping holes or questions unanswered, because it's often too late to go back and replay the conversation once the interview has ended."

—Claudia A. Sampson, Founder/Managing Director, LEEDS Coaching

"Just about any problem in your job history can be overcome if you know how to talk about it in the right terms. A combination of candor and forward focus in answering questions about a layoff, time away from your career to parent, or even a termination, can turn any negative into a positive. Look for the lessons learned and focus on where you want to go, rather than where you've been, and you'll be golden."

—Elizabeth Cronise McLaughlin, CEO/Lead Executive Coach, Elizabeth Cronise McLaughlin Coaching

"During the interview process stay true to yourself. Don't compromise by trying to become someone you are not in order to please the interviewer. Otherwise, in the end, who is benefiting?"

—Gretchen A. Grubel, Vice President Human Resources, Hourglass Cosmetics

"Be nice to everyone. When I was a recruiter for United Airlines, I often ran into aspiring Flight Attendants in the Ladies Room. The ones who smiled, held the door for me and generally had a pleasant energy (even though they had no idea I would soon be interviewing them) were ahead of the game."

—Linda DeCarlo, Linda DeCarlo Training and Coaching

"It is essential to honestly sell WHY you are the best person for the position. Employers seek knowledge, experience and organizational fit to add or replace headcount. Present your responses in a S.T.A.R (Situation,Task, Action & Results) format and your value will be seen."

—Teauna Upshaw MBA, PHR, Workforce Initiatives

"Generally speaking there are two types of employees in the world. The first type is 'Willing.' Ask them to go from point A to point B and they usually do. When these employees reach point B, they'll report back and ask for more direction. That's good, but not great. The second type is 'Eager.' Ask these self-starters to go from point A to point B and you'll almost immediately get their thinking and related plans on how and why they will go to point C, D, E, etc. Employers covet this type of employee because they tend to get important things done with minimal direction. When interviewing, it's critical that you ask questions and provide examples that clearly put you in the 'Eager' category."

—David Almeda, Chief People Officer, Kronos Incorporated

"While knowing your audience is an obvious suggestion it goes further than just research. For example, when you come to HT headquarters for an interview and we offer you a drink, take it! We are a beverage company, we want to know that you want to drink our beverages!"

—Debra Schwartz, VP, Human Resources, HONEST TEA, Inc.

"It's true that 'You never get a second chance to make a first impression.' So be genuine, but realize that this is essentially The Show. You've practiced, you've done all your work behind the scenes, you have your resume, you've studied your script, and now you're on stage and it's time to perform. And there's a lot riding on this performance."

—Reid Styles, VP of Human Resources, The Franklin Institute

"Of course you should negotiate your salary and get what you're worth. But in the end, it's not just about the money. Do you have a good boss? Do you have a good commute? Is this your dream job? Are you doing something worthwhile? Money is just part of that equation."

—Jim Hopkinson, The Salary Tutor, author of *Salary Tutor: Learn the Salary Negotiation Secrets No One Ever Taught You*

"Ask questions about how decisions are made and what gets cut when budgets get tight. The answers tell you about culture and priorities of the company and its leaders. Your contentment and engagement will depend on the alignment of these to your own."

—Darin Seeley, Sr. Manager, Human Resources and Talent Acquisition, Black Hills Corporation

"Lean in. Show interest and engage your interviewer by leaning in to respond to questions."

—Myles Miller, CEO& Founder, SUCCESSHQ

"I wish that all job interviewees knew that their primary objective in a job interview is to make the interviewer look good. The interviewer has a job to do: find the best candidate for the position at hand. You need to give the interviewer a reason to put his/her neck on the line and champion your candidacy with upper management. Therefore, it's crucial that your answers to interview questions be memorable and quotable in addition to being spot-on. If your interviewer can't recall what you said, he or she (literally) won't be able to present you to the next tier of decision-makers."

—Joseph Terach, CEO, Resume Deli

"It's important to view yourself as a product. Make sure you are packaged properly (proper interview dress and grooming) and then market yourself effectively. Walk in with compelling marketing materials (resume, LinkedIn Profile, portfolio, etc.) and be prepared to serve as your own salesperson. Do your homework on the organization, be confidant in what you have to offer, and then show why the organization needs you."

—Michelle A. Riklan, Managing Director, Riklan Resources

"Talk about what your strengths are, how you've used those strengths to impact your organization and how you will use your strengths to provide value to this new team."

—Sandy Lewis, VP Human Resources, Advanced Liquid Logic

"The one thing all interviewees should know is that 'Confidence is King.' When you go into an interview with confidence, we interviewers sense that — and why wouldn't we want someone on our team who knows they can get the job done because they are the best at it!"

—Dana Harris, President, DMarie & Co.

"Be honest and do not over sell yourself. Humility will be appreciated and rewarded."

          —Jean-Claude Lalumiere, Senior HR Executive

"Job interviews can be very stressful for some people, especially if you depend on getting this job. So prepare for the interview by creating a compliment journal. Write down five compliments about yourself each day for thirty days. This builds your confidence, and when you are confident, the interviewer will see that. Your stress levels will also go down, because you'll know that you can handle the interview and show that you're able to do the job well."

      —Leo Willcocks, Author of *DeStress to Success, Solving Stress and Winning Big In Relationships, Wealth and Life Itself*

"Don't ever appear desperate or overly anxious to land the role. It can be detected by the interviewer very easily. You have to be confident to the point of feeling that if this job is a fit, fine, but if not, it's no big deal."

      —Gary Glandon, Chief Human Resources Officer, Rogers Corporation

"A job interview is not about you — it's about the company and what it needs you to do. Study the company, its market, and its competition in advance, so that you have an idea about how you can contribute to its success."

      —Alfred Poor, Speaker, Success Mentor, Author of *7 Success Secrets That Every College Student Needs to Know!*

"Interviewers are looking for reasons to disqualify a candidate, and a common mistake interviewees make is to give too much information or believe they have to 'tell the truth, the whole truth and nothing but the truth.' Here's an example: If they ask, 'Are you open to relocation?' answer, 'Yes, for the right growth opportunity and career track I am very open to relocation,' even if you don't think you want to relocate. If you can't get your head around what I'm suggesting, then go with what will satisfy your ethics and morals. Just know that, if that company relocates people as part of their career development, you've just handed the job to someone else."

—Ed Chaffin, Founder/President,
The UnCommon Leadership Institute

"Know that no matter how qualified you are for the role (in terms of experience, education, skills, etc.) you need to be 'likable.' If you're not, its much simpler to pass on you for the next person. So be prompt, polite, be yourself; listen and engage with the interviewer."

—Debbie Mitchell, Human Resources Executive

"Self awareness is key to finding a job. That plays into leveraging one's passion in the interviewing process. Passion (emotion) ultimately drives performance."

—Winsor Jenkins, VP, Human Resources,
Northwest Pipe Company

"If a candidate is truly excited about working for my company, I expect that they will become as knowledgeable about it as possible; but most candidates do very little research. Your interview dialog should incorporate knowledge that you've gained from: the company's web site ("About Us", "Our History" and "Career Opportunities" or "Employment" tabs); financial analysts' reports (if a public company); press releases and news stories about the organization; and LinkedIn profiles of people who work in your target department."

—Mike Perry, President, Szarka Financial

"Applying for positions is not a numbers game. Stop applying for any and all positions, and just focus on the opportunities that you're genuinely interested in. Track when you apply, when you hear back, and when you interview. There is nothing more frustrating than calling an applicant and having them ask what position you're calling about!"

—Samantha Lambert, Director of Human Resources,
Blue Fountain Media

"Come up with 3-5 talking points, and think about how you can fit them into your responses to typical interview questions. If you feel nervous when you enter the room say something like, 'If I seem nervous, it's just because I'm so happy to be here.' And ask your interviewer, 'Do you like working here?' Try to have fun with the interview process; it's your opportunity to find a job you will love."

—Jenny Gallagher, Co-Founder, Business Success

"The primary 'must know' is the specific need (hot button) the company is experiencing at present and how you above all other candidates can be a solution for that need. The key to selling yourself as the answer to their needs is to be able to clearly and concisely articulate your skills, knowledge, achievements/results and competencies. And to do this, you must do your research on the company, industry and sector."

—Paul Vagadori, VP Human Resources, Lahlouh

"Only apply for professional roles in which you can position yourself as an expert! In the pharmaceutical industry, many advertised roles receive numerous applications, and to dramatically increase your chances of being hired, this is crucial."

—Dr. Samuel Dyer, Chairman of the Board, Medical Science Liaison Society, Author of *The Medical Science Liaison Career Guide: How to Break Into Your First Role*

"At the end of the day, an interview is a conversation between two people to determine best fit. It shouldn't be feared. Go into it confidently, because you have as much to gain from it as the hiring company does."

—Laurie Berenson, President & Certified Master Resume Writer, Sterling Career Concepts, LLC

"Interviewee's should do their research on the company and its culture and know the current news about them. It's also important to read the job description and tailor your answers to what the company is looking for in the role. Make it a no brainer for the company to see the job fit!"

—Heidi Ferolito, Human Resources Director, Talent Acquisition and Retention, World Travel Holdings

"Ask questions that show evidence of your research on the organization. Suggest something that has the potential to bring in business or add revenue in an innovative way that has not yet been considered. The former shows initiative and the latter creativity and innovation, all of which are high in importance."

—Lynda Zugec, Managing Director, The Workforce Consultants

"I wish job candidates knew that they would have better results if they were bold enough to stand out. Don't just show up for the interview, ask for the job. Interview the interviewer. You have as much power over who gets this job as they do."

—Ramon Santillan, Chief Interview Consultant, Persuasive Interview

"I wish all interviewees knew the hiring manager was trying to solve a problem, instead of filling an open position. When you're trying to fill an open position, you concentrate on the requirements listed on the position description. When you're trying to solve a problem, you ask questions that clarify the problem and test the solutions that have been attempted. When an interviewee offers a solution to the hiring manager's problem, the hiring manager starts to feel confident that the person will be able to do the job that was designed to fix that problem."

—Tom Gottfreid, President, Fresh Start of Illinois

"I would encourage candidates to prepare for the interview, and research the organization and the individuals with whom you'll be meeting. Identify good questions in advance to ask of those you're interviewing with to help them determine if you would be a good fit in the organization."

— Katherine Neverdousky, VP, Human Resources at American Heart Association (AHA)

"You should be interviewing the company as stringently as the company interviews you. Be honest about your strengths and weaknesses, and understand whether or not you can be successful at this job. If not, you should walk away from the interview opportunity."

— Lori Kleiman, SPHR, Author of *Fire HR Now!*

"Know the company! Every good interviewer will ask what you have learned about the company in your research, so be sure to have done more work than just spending 10 minutes on the web site. Read press releases, read other web sites about them, buy the product, go through the sales process...really do your part to know the company and the product. It will serve you well."

—Evelyn Walter, GPHR, VP Human Resources, Inspirato

"You have to know yourself and be able to communicate who you are and what you know in a clear, precise manner. This includes being able to tell someone what behaviors and values you possess that make you a perfect candidate for the job."
—Parker Geiger, CEO, CHUVA group

"Come prepared to tell personal stories that demonstrate you can do the job. When candidates talk in the abstract or theoretically, it is hard to gauge if they can deliver on what they are saying. Stories about what you've done allow the interviewer to measure concretely, as well as assess your cultural fit by understanding what you would do differently in hindsight, how you worked with others, and your ability to take ownership of results."

—Jason Henrichs, Managing Director, Startup Institute

"The most overlooked and most needed piece of paper is a contact card (formerly called a business card). A person looking for a position cannot be constantly handing out resumes. You need to be able to leave your information with every person you meet."

—Kathy Condon, Communications Author, Speaker, and Trainer

"One of the most important elements of an interview is for the candidate to be able to describe their knowledge of the employer and how they can contribute to the success of the organization utilizing their skills, knowledge and energy."

—John P. Nester, Human Resources Manager

"I wish all job interviewees knew what to do with their hands during a job interview. Too often, I see people who stay static, hands on knees, because they don't know what posture to adopt. Think of your hands as a way to give life to the words you utter, to express your passion and your motivation. Be active!"

—Kelly Hadous, President, Win the Room

"We often see students who are applying for internships go into their interviews rattling off classes they've taken or listing specific software programs in which they're fluent, but forgetting to talk about what makes THEM the best candidate for the internship. Are you persuasive, easy-going, articulate, a go-getter? What differentiates you from your classmates who took the exact same classes and know the exact same software?"

—Val Hunt Beerbower, Co-Owner, DaytonINTERNS

"I wish all job interviewees knew that you need to be ready to answer three questions:

♦ Can you do the job? — Strengths (not just technical skills)
♦ Will you love the job? — Motivation (what makes you happy)
♦ Can we tolerate working with you? — Fit (are you going to fit well in this culture)"

—Cindy Allen-Stuckey, CEO, Making Performance Matter

"Every interviewee should have questions for the interviewer/team. Remember, they are screening you for the role and you are screening them to make sure the company is the right fit for you. Make sure you find out what their culture and onboarding process is. This is essential, as research has proven that the reason new employees leave in the first year is cultural fit."

—Eileen Timmins, Ph.D., Global HR Executive, Aingilin, LLC

"Come in with a great question, because they will ask if you have one. Saying no shows that you are not prepared. Then, quite frankly, ask for the job! See yourself working at this company and picture in your mind that this interviewer likes you as a candidate. Be the best, because you know you are. There is no one else in the entire world that is just like you!"

—Dr. Michael Provitera, Author of *Mastering Self-Motivation: Preparing Yourself for Personal Excellence*

"In health care, we don't care that you love people and do irrelevant volunteer work. We want to know that you're clinically competent and work well with others."

—Nick Angelis, CRNA, MSN, Author of *How to Succeed in Anesthesia School (And RN, PA, or Med School)*

"The follow-up letter is absolutely critical following a job interview. As a hiring manager, if I do not get one, I take it for granted that the interviewee was not really enthusiastic about the position."

—Mario Almonte, Managing Partner, Herman & Almonte Public Relations

"I wish that job interviewees understood that you need to answer questions by telling better stories, and not just giving one or two work answers. People engage with a good story, so prepare stories for the common questions that are asked, like 'Tell me about a time you had to deal with a difficult situation.' Be ready to go right into the story when you get the question. This gives you more authority, and shows confidence."

—Vernon Ross, Business Coach

"The best questions show not just an interest in the job but an interest in helping the company accomplish its goals.
For example:
♦ 'What would the perfect employee for this job look like for you?'
♦ 'In the best of all possible worlds, what would you like me to accomplish for you? In three months? In a year? In five years?' "

—Barry Maher, Barry Maher & Associates

"I wish every candidate knew that being as real and honest about who you are is a much better strategy than trying to be who you think the interviewer wants you to be."

—David MacWilliams, Regional Director, HR, McGladrey

Learn More

Whatever aspect of public speaking or communications you want to explore further, you'll find actionable ideas, insights, and inspiration at my web site, *Speak Up for Success*.

> Find more information about **HOW TO ACE A JOB INTERVIEW** — including in-depth interviews with six seasoned interviewers — in this *Speak Up for Success* blog post about **JOB INTERVIEWING**:

SpeakUpForSuccess.com/category/job-interviews

> Want further tips on conquering **PUBLIC SPEAKING FEAR**? Here's where to go for articles and encouragement:

SpeakUpForSuccess.com/category/fear-of-public-speaking

> Would you like to understand **YOUR PUBLIC SPEAKING PERSONALITY**? Find out if you're a Reliable, Helper, Improver, or Experiencer, and how the answer can make you a better communicator:

SpeakUpForSuccess.com/category/your-public-speaking-personality

> And if your goal is to **BE A WORLD-CLASS PUBLIC SPEAKER** — or just to speak with confidence in meetings, networking events, etc. — my fast-paced, user-friendly workbook, *SPEAK LIKE YOURSELF...No, Really! Follow Your Strengths and Skills to Great Public Speaking* is available in paper or ebook:

http://amzn.to/QpQ7oA

Praise for
SPEAK LIKE YOURSELF... No, Really!
Follow Your Strengths and Skills
to Great Public Speaking

"If you want to get started as a speaker or improve your presentation skills, this book is for you. Jezra's explanations, tips and examples are clear and easy to understand. She has a natural warmth and down-to-earth style that'll make you feel like she's your own private coach."

—Dana Rubin, Speechwriter and Director, New York
Speechwriter's Roundtable

"Is there anything new under the sun for public speakers since Demosthenes addressed the roaring sea with pebbles in his mouth? Maybe not; but if you're looking for a clear understanding of the subject, presented in an engaging manner, look no further."

—Charles di Cagno, Director, Public Speaking Center of NY

"I've presented more than 30 keynote speeches this year, and the feedback and advice I received from Jezra was invaluable. Now, with the publication of her book, so many will have the opportunity to benefit by simply reading and putting her easy-to-employ advice to use."

—Ted Rubin, Social Marketing Strategist,
Keynote Speaker, Brand Evangelist, Acting CMO of Brand
Innovators, and Co-Author of *Return on Relationship*

"No matter what your position, no matter what your job, we all have to communicate—and this book will take you to the next level of success."

—Anne Loehr, Author, Executive Coach, and Keynote Speaker
(named "Generational Guru" by *The Washington Post*)

"A must-read for any business professional. Jezra is a speaker coaching guru, and this book will boost your public speaking skills, whether you're a beginner or an expert."

—Jeremy Masters, Founder & Managing Partner, Worklogix

"Jezra's advice and wisdom make public speaking easy and authentic. She'll help you create an experience that not only meets your goals but is enjoyable, too!"

—Adelaide Lancaster, Business Coach, Co-Founder of
In Good Company Workplaces, and Co-Author of
*The Big Enough Company: How Women Can Build Great
Businesses and Happier Lives*

Jezra Kaye

Jezra Kaye — acclaimed speaker coach, seminar leader, keynote speaker, and president of **Speak Up for Success** — is a former Fortune 500 speechwriter who shows individuals and organizations around the U.S. and the world how to present themselves and their ideas with power, passion, authenticity, and ease.

A former jazz singer and bandleader, Jezra is also the author of *Speak Like Yourself... No, Really! Follow Your Strengths and Skills to Great Public Speaking*, the co-author of *Managing the Unmanageable: How to Motivate Even the Most Unruly Employee*, and the author of a novel, *The Tattooed Heart*, and a book of poetry, *Kicking*. She lives and works in Brooklyn, New York.

To learn more about Jezra's Skype or in-person speaker coaching, or customized workshops and keynote speeches, visit SpeakUpforSuccess.com

Made in the USA
Charleston, SC
15 August 2014